SOUL *TO* SOLE

SOUL *TO* SOLE
THE VIEWS FROM THE SHOES

AUTHOR

CAROLYN EVAUGHN KNOWLES

iUniverse LLC
Bloomington

SOUL TO SOLE
THE VIEWS FROM THE SHOES

iUniverse books may be ordered through booksellers or by contacting:

iUniverse
1663 Liberty Drive
Bloomington, IN 47403
www.iuniverse.com
1-800-Authors (1-800-288-4677)

ISBN: 978-1-4917-3292-2 (sc)
ISBN: 978-1-4917-3294-6 (hc)
ISBN: 978-1-4917-3293-9 (e)

Library of Congress Control Number: 2014907780

Printed in the United States of America.

iUniverse rev. date: 06/09/2014

CONTENTS

PART III

SUMMER'S TIME

PART IV

THE SHOE STORE
Contributors

PART V

FITTED SHOES

PREFACE

As a product of a single-parent family, I can relate to those women and girls who wonder what it would have been like to have had a "real" father in the home. To have had a dad that served God and loved and respected himself; a man under whose protection, provision, and love they could have flourished. These delicate flowers can only wish to have had a father that would have willingly sacrificed his own existence to serve as the cornerstone of his family's dreams and aspirations. I can relate to the scars that such an absence leaves—wounds that impact the quality of relationships we establish and maintain with men. My early view of the opposite sex was so negative that I told myself I would never get married. However, as God would have it, He placed the right man in my life that shows an "authentic" love for God, for our daughter, and for me. He even has space in his heart to love humankind.

Having a strong Christian mother was critical in my developmental years. I also benefitted from having other women in my life who shared with me their time, talent, and treasures, helping to mold me into the woman I am today. One woman in particular, Alice Gantt, was my she-ro. Although she passed away in 1991, she will always hold a special place in my heart. She thought the sun rose and set upon me. She was my caregiver for many years and loved me as if I was her own daughter. We were so close that I referred to her as my godmother.

Relationships among women can be beautiful, but they can also be challenging. In life there are relationships between mothers and daughters; godmothers and goddaughters; sisters, aunts, nieces, cousins, girlfriends, girl enemies, colleagues, extended relatives, and associates. You can imagine the dynamics that can exist between members of any of these groups.

In November 2010, my mother came to live with my husband and me. She previously lived with us for temporary periods of time, but this was now a permanent arrangement. Our lives would significantly change. You see, our one and only child had completed college and was blessed to immediately find employment in her field of study. Therefore, she did not have to return home as so many graduates do. Also, our one and only dog died in 2000, and we decided against replacing him. Our home was now empty but filled with just us. Although we missed both daughter and dog, we were able to enjoy having an empty nest for more than 10 years. We could come and go as we pleased, not having to be concerned about anyone or anything—except one another.

As I began reflecting on this time in my life, I realized that a story had been developing over the years that needed to be told. Initially, the book would share perspectives from three generations of women: my mother (traditionalist), my daughter (millennial), and me (baby boomer). However, as these nearly four years have passed, the Lord continued to speak to my heart and mind. Thus, *Soul to Sole* evolved into an amazing story with prolific accounts from several contributors, one of which is a man. That singular male is my husband of 35 years, Gil. He gets to tell his story about his relationships with my mom, our daughter, and me. It's quite a treat, as he tells his "Views from Polished Shoes," hoping that his story can inspire others to consider expanding their circle of love.

It is our prayer that *Soul to Sole* touches someone who may be traveling the road that one of us has walked. We hope that our wisdom, guidance, and raw truths help women and girls to know that through Christ, all things are possible.

In today's world, it seems to be all about the "Benjamins" and all about "me." However, there are many of us who actually care about more than money and self-preservation. The storytellers in this book want to show that there are ties that bind us together as women and girls. We experience many of the same life challenges that affect our physical, emotional, financial, spiritual, and social wellbeing. Through *Soul to Sole,* we want to show the world that we are blessed and highly favored of the Lord. We want our stories to be a godsend to others, especially women and girls, so they may discover the strength that lies within that propels them forward in a mighty way.

ACKNOWLEDGEMENTS

This book has taken nearly four years to write and has awakened many different emotions. There have been feelings of love, joy, and happiness, as well as bitterness, sadness, and frustration. There have been challenges in relationships as well as obstacles that at times seemed insurmountable. But, God always restored my soul. I want to acknowledge and thank the following persons who contributed to this work:

- Gilbert Knowles
- Summer Knowles
- Lucille Floyd
- Mabel Jones Matthews
- Abdual Lindsey, cover design
- Natryia Rampey, cover photo credit, Lucille Floyd and Carolyn Knowles
- Manuel Torres, cover photo credit, Summer Knowles
- Steven McGill
- Joyce Garrett
- Gale Rolle
- Delisia Matthews
- Crystal Gay
- Jyia Lindsey
- Josephine Hamilton
- Tamika Lynn

- Cassandra Brumby
- Claudette Davis
- Rosalie Randall
- Lydia Rainer, reader
- Brigitte Maxey, editor

DEDICATION

Soul to Sole: The Views from the Shoes is dedicated to my husband of 35 years, Lieutenant Colonel (Retired, U. S. Army) Gilbert A. Knowles. He has definitely been and continues to be my "soul mate." He is the father of our beautiful and talented daughter, Summer. He and I have committed to being there for each other, through thick and thin. As in any marriage, we have had our share of challenges, but God continues to deliver us. How many men would do for their mothers-in-law what Gil does for my mom? His love for me extends beyond me . . . to my mom . . . to the point where he has become her primary caregiver. Gil works from home and is the one who prepares my mom's breakfast every morning; he is the one who takes her to medical appointments; he is the one who religiously organizes her medications and ensures she takes them. Yes, he is the one.

Because my commute to work is almost two hours one way, Gil actually drives me to work each day so that I can get a little more sleep on the road. On the weekends, I try to give him a break. However, without his commitment to me and his love for me, we could not take care of my mom as we do.

Soul to Sole is about our spiritual and physical walk through life. Gil has a chapter in this book, which talks about his "Views from Polished Shoes." I thank God for bringing Gil into my life. He is a man of God, who shows "real" support and "real" love. He is truly authentic and I love him forever.

INTRODUCTION

Throughout your life, you will try on many different types of shoes and you will actually choose to wear some of them. *Soul to Sole: The Views from the Shoes* present shoe analogies that inspire you to find the shoe that fits. It encourages you to find the shoe that makes you feel comfortable. It moves you to find the shoe that supports the different seasons of your life. This introspective book takes you on a wonderful journey into the hearts and souls of several women as they discuss some of their life experiences, which have made them into the women they are today. It provides strong emotions as you ride on the rollercoaster of life that gives you the thrill of victory and the agony of defeat. We initially present the perspectives of three women from three different generations: one from the Traditionalist Generation (1900—1945); one from the Baby Boomer Generation (1946—1964); and one from the Millennial Generation (1981—2000). As the stories continue, you will read about additional experiences from other women who have traveled different roads. They share their *Views from the Shoes* so that others can relate to and benefit from their encounters. The women in this book describe how they navigated the roads that led to their current stations. They share their mountain highs and their valley lows. They highlight the importance of pursuing their passion. Theirs are stories that show where love abounded and life unfolded; where determination persisted and success prevailed; where the distance was run and the victory won. Through it all, they learned how to lean and depend on God.

Soul to Sole: The Views from the Shoes contains revelations of the mind and heart. It describes the holistic woman as she endures, embraces, and overcomes the physical, emotional, financial, social, and spiritual challenges of life. It also focuses on revelations from the "sole," as it reflects upon the consequences of our daily walk. As a baby, we have to go through several stages before we can control where we go. First, we learn to use our knees to crawl. Then, we start to use our feet to stand up and move out, taking baby steps that tend to satisfy our innate curiosity. To protect our soft and tender feet, we wear cute and comfortable socks and booties. During this period, we have no responsibilities, except to do what babies do: eat, sleep, cry, pee, and poop. We expect others to take care of our every need. However, this stage does not last very long.

As we grow through the terrible twos, the terrific threes, the ferocious fours, and the furious fives, our feet start to take us to additional places of exploration and discovery. We are more cognizant of our surroundings, as the people, places, and things in our lives begin to take on new meanings. The "soles" of our shoes must now take on a tougher task, for we are now beginning to walk on rougher ground. The soft, cute, and comfortable booty can no longer serve as our major source of foot cover because our need for protection has become greater.

Pre-kindergarten through 12th grade is a period of even more growth. Our bodies stretch up and out, with shoe sizes reaching their peaks. Our minds expand, demonstrating vast intellectual and conceptual capabilities. Our emotions explode with a greater need for association and socialization. Our desires for worldly possessions become a driver, determining our need for financial gain and stability. Our inner spirits serve as our conscience, allowing us to discern right from wrong, good from evil, and ethical from unethical. By now, we are already walking on a path. For some of us, the road may be smooth and wide, with few detours along the way. For others, the road may be rocky and narrow, with obstacles and hurdles to overcome every day. However, for most of us, this walk will be a combination of the two. We can choose to wear beautiful flats, pumps, or high heels on the roads that are easy to tread—days that are sunny and bright. Or, we can choose to wear practical boots or orthopedic shoes on the roads that are hard to travel—days that are dark and dreary.

As we continue our journey through our 20's, 30's, 40's, and 50's, even to our 60's, 70's and beyond, our feet will take us through the ups and downs of life. There will be times when we will choose to wear high fashion and designer shoes, depicting a spirit of fun and folly. There will also be times when we will choose to wear bargain shoes, demonstrating our need for comfort and practicality.

This book uses shoe stories to vividly describe the mindset and thought processes that girls and women may develop as they progress from baby booties to flats; from sandals to tennis shoes; from ankle boots to riding boots; or from pumps to stilettos. It addresses the need for orthopedic shoes that lack appeal but provide repair. As we defend our "souls" from hurt and our "soles" from pain, we are writing our own chapter of *Soul to Sole: The Views from the Shoes*.

Part I of the book focuses on my mom, Lucille. Because she is senior in age, she uses the oral tradition to pass her story to me and I translate it for us. If it is perceived as grammatically incorrect, that's alright because it is what it is. The time spent acquiring this information from my mom proved to be a labor of love. We hope this book is a blessing to all who read it.

Part II focuses on my story. I reveal the road I chose on which to journey through life. I speak candidly on how my choices made the difference in my rise out of poverty. I uncover the challenges and threats to my successes that allowed me to be a victor instead of a victim.

Part III focuses on Summer, where she talks about aspects of her life that will inspire the millennial generation and even younger groups. However, her story reveals an authenticity, which can be appreciated by all audiences.

Part IV begins the transition to contributors, which starts with Gil. He describes his relationship with the three women, who are his wife, daughter, and mother-in-law. He provides a raw truth about his *Views from Polished Shoes*. It continues with a collection of stories from selected women, who are strong daughters of God. They share aspects of their lives in hope of strengthening readers with their wisdom and their woes. They provide a variety of scenarios that are thought provoking and relevant.

Part V returns focus to my story where I impart the importance of living life to the fullest and putting God first. I recall how I gained the wisdom to learn from the highs and lows of others journeys. I pray that this section empowers the reader to find shoes that perfectly fit travel that is uniquely theirs, with the understanding they may have to change styles from time to time.

Get ready to meet trailblazers who have cleared the pathways for us. Prepare to embrace their spirits as you connect with the heart of your own story. Get ready to understand why no woman should be an island unto herself. Know that there are ties that bind us in so many ways. Together we can share; together we can care; and together we can stand as strong women in Christ. Please don't forget to feed your soul with the fruit of the spirit: love, joy, peace, kindness, goodness, gentleness, faithfulness, patience, and discipline. Then, find your shoes and wear them well!

But if we walk in the light, as he is in the
light, we have fellowship one with one another,
and the blood of Jesus Christ his son cleanseth
us from all sin.

1 John 1:7 (King James Version)

Part I

September's Child

September's Child

By
Lucille Floyd

September's child has seen many years,
through many doubts and many fears.
God has been my only shield,
for He is the driver at my steering wheel.

My body runs to and fro,
like a machine, as fast as it can go.
So, thank you God for one more day,
to worship you in my feeble way.

It took a long time for me to learn,
how much you love me and are concerned.
By your hands I am fed—and I thank you Lord,
for giving me bread.

Please dear God, help my pocket book to grow,
so that I can give just a little bit more.
For in your word I do believe,
it is better to give than to receive.

I am your September's child, somewhat battered and worn;
but never from you will I be torn.
I will stay on the battlefield and fight my fight;
I will fight my plight with all my might.
And when my time has finally come,
this September's child will walk around heaven
with a mighty song and a mighty hum.

CHAPTER 1

The Unveiling

**"Take 'um . . . Take 'um! We don't want 'um!"
These are the horrible words spewed at the
newborn child.**

It is 1924 in Charleston, South Carolina. The scene is a small, one bedroom shack, where a "girl baby" is about to be born. She would be the first child allowed to live. You see, her mother had been pregnant before, but each time she had to get rid of the baby before it lived. Her mother did not work and she was the "bread winner" for the family. Therefore, each time she got pregnant, her mother made her abort the baby. However, this time, neighbors said, "Enough is enough! You will not kill this one." Therefore, when the time came, they summoned for Miss Susie, the elderly local midwife, who delivered this new soul into the world.

After she cut the umbilical cord, Miss Susie put the baby in a rocking chair. Excrement from the placenta formed a dark veil over the baby's small face. Miss Susie immediately spun into action, cutting the net and removing the waste material from the baby's body. This was the dramatic entry of Lucille into the world, which was a harbinger of things to come.

Her birth mother and grandmother chose not to keep baby Lucille. So what now? Crying inconsolably, Lucille captured the heart of Miss Susie and thus began a mother-daughter relationship, as Miss Susie decided to raise Lucille as her own.

What could have been a tragedy became a miracle. In essence, what the devil meant for bad, God used for good. Who would have thought the right person, with the right skills, would show up at the right time to fulfill the will of God, which was life, and not death, for Lucille. Apparently, Miss Susie was on a mission from God that brought together a total stranger and a helpless child.

Lucille's Voice and Vernacular

My name is Lucille Brown; Lucille Brown Bennett; Lucille Brown Bennett Floyd. But it could have been Lucille Morgan; Lucille Morgan Bennett; Lucille Morgan Bennett Floyd. Or, it could have been Lucille Flynn; Lucille Flynn Bennett; Lucille Flynn Bennett Floyd. You wonder how could one person have so many possible names? Well, I am glad you asked. I was born to an unwed mother whose last name was Morgan. However, my adopted mother's last name was Brown. My birth father's last name was Flynn. My first husband's last name was Bennett and my second husband's last name was Floyd. The name that I carry to this day is Lucille B. Floyd and the "B" is for Brown. That is because I truly value that "B" for it represents the "B" from my adopted mother, Susan Brown. **She chose me.**

My adopted parents were great. Stephen Brown was my adopted dad, but he died when I was a small child. I do not remember much about him. Susan Brown was a wonderful mom. She had a son named

Henry, who was much older than me. I saw him as a father figure because Susan was really too old to actually be my mother.

Susan Brown was a strong, brave, and loving woman, who earned most of her living as a seamstress. I can remember how she made all my clothes, as well as suits for men. We initially lived in the city of Charleston, where I was born but later moved to her hometown of White Hall, SC. Mom left Charleston with me and her two grandchildren—Willie Mae and Allen—and never looked back.

White Hall was considered the deep, dark country. Willie Mae, Allen, and I had never seen live animals and were frightened by the cows, hogs, chickens, and snakes. When mom had to go into the woods to get kindling to keep us warm, Allen and I would cry until she returned. We innocently called the cows and hogs "big" and "little" dogs.

Mom had no stove. She cooked and kept us warm by a fireplace, called the chimney. She had to go into the woods to cut pieces of limbs that had fallen off trees. We all sat in front of the chimney to keep warm. We had never seen a big fire like that because we were used to a cooking stove. We thought it was strange that mom had to cook in the chimney.

Willie Mae was the youngest but the bravest. She never would cry and would yell after us to be quiet. I was the oldest and the biggest cry baby. Since Allen and Willie Mae were Susan's grandchildren, they were only in the country for a short time before they went back to the city to their mom. But I had to stay. At night, when mom would go to prayer meeting, she had to carry me on her back because I used to see things that she could not see, such as ghosts, and I was too frightened to walk alone. Mom would put me on her back and I would keep my eyes closed until we got home.

When I was with my mom in White Hall, SC, money was tight. As a child, I didn't process what it meant to be without so I would ask for things like all the other kids. Mom never told me no. When she didn't have money, she would catch one of her chickens, take it to the grocery store and sell it. She would then give the money to me to spend as I wanted.

I had never seen a live chicken and I was afraid of it. Why? Because one day I was sitting on the steps and a big chicken, which they called a rooster, hurt me. I used to have sores on my legs and that big rooster came up to me and pecked right into my sore and down came the blood. I ran into the house screaming. My mom cleaned me up. That left a lasting impression. Although I will eat all the chicken that I can get, I will never hold a live chicken in my hands.

I started school in the country without a birth certificate and I did not get one until I was eighteen. I was always smart in school. I remember there were three of us who always got to keep our seats in the front of the class because our grades were always very good. I never learned how to dance, ride a bike or skate, but I did enjoy playing games like hide and seek, jump rope, and hop scotch. As much as I loved my mom, I really did not like living in the country. It was so dark and scary. I kept asking my mom to let me go back to the city to live with my Aunt (her sister). Finally, when I was about twelve years old, she agreed and I moved back to Charleston.

Although I missed my mom, I was happy to be back in the city. I started at a new school and made some new friends. My aunt was pretty strict. All I could do was go to school and to church activities. I served on the usher board from the age of twelve and I also enjoyed singing. Sometimes my aunt allowed me to play at my friends' homes, but I had to be home before dark.

Sometimes there were fights in school, but I was always a scare-dy cat and never had a fight with anyone in my life. I will tell you this: I had many a good runs getting away from flying fists. When I saw a fight coming up, I would head in the other direction. I've never been one to witness a fight either. I had a cousin who was very nosy and would stick her mouth into every action at school. Someone would tell me my cousin was fighting on Hanover Street. I said, "OK," but then I would walk on Nassau Street, which was the next street over. If I got the message she was fighting on Nassau Street, I would walk to Hanover Street. I was just not one to fight, but I would go and get help—I would not be that help.

My aunt provided a loving home and stable environment for me but as the years went by and I began to get older, I realized more than ever that Susan Brown was too old to be my natural mother. I had always heard rumors about a woman who was supposedly my birth mother. Finally, curiosity stepped in and took over. I was determined to find out if there was any truth to the rumors. I began questioning my mom and my aunt and finally learned the truth. The stranger, Hattie, was indeed my mother. However, in the same breath that whispered her name, I was forbidden from making any attempts to see her.

As with all things forbidden, my interest peaked. After receiving confirmation that Hattie was my mother, I could not think of anything else, except meeting Hattie and getting to know her. I had so many questions. I had seen this beautiful woman in the neighborhood, walking to and from work. I thought we looked alike, as we both had big brown eyes and long black hair. Now, I couldn't wait to make a connection, or better yet, a love connection.

One day, I worked up the nerve to go to Hattie's house. I nervously walked up to the door and knocked. Hattie answered graciously. There was an immediate bond between us. We sat for a short while and talked, but I had to be on my way, knowing I would be in trouble if my mom or my aunt knew of my detour.

Hattie was overcome with happiness knowing that I did not hate her and actually wanted to know her. She then decided to also pursue seeing me by trying to visit me at my aunt's house. However, my mom and my aunt were not having it! They never forgot the way Hattie left me for dead in that old rocking chair. My mom and aunt wanted no part of Hattie and wanted me to have no part of her either. Hattie was determined to visit me. Each day after work she would try to come by the house but would be met with rocks and stones thrown by my aunt who wanted to deter her. Many days she would be bloodied from the stones, but she continued to try.

I was in the middle of an uncomfortable situation. I greatly loved my mom and my aunt, as they were the only family I had ever known. However, I had a real desire to establish a relationship with my birth mother as well as my half brothers and sisters. Therefore, I decided to not let Hattie continue to get stoned. To ensure we were able to see each other, I decided to make Hattie's house a stop along my way from school each day. This seemed to be a reasonable solution. Hattie and I talked about many things, including why she was forced to abandon me. My heart was touched by the sadness and genuine sorrow in Hattie's voice as she told her story, explaining the events that led to that terrible decision. This was the beginning of a loving friendship—not between a mother and daughter but more between friends.

While I was living with my aunt, my friend Louise and I were very close. Sometimes I was allowed to go and play with her at her house. She lived next door to this boy that I liked. But, I was too shy to talk to him. Louise would strike up a conversation with him for me, but I wouldn't say anything because I was so scared. As time went by, he and I became friends. I was then about fifteen and he wanted to marry me. I wanted to marry him too, but my mom was totally against it. She said I was too young. And, since he was a few years older than me, my mom thought he was too old for me. He decided to go into the military to wait for me to come of age. However, when he returned from his tour of duty, I had messed up. I got into a relationship with someone else, got pregnant and ended up dropping out of school. I then needed a birth certificate to get married. As I mentioned earlier, I never needed a birth certificate to get into school, so I never had one.

I married Leroy Bennett and after the baby was born I got a job at the American Tobacco Company, called the "Cigar Factory." I worked there for twenty seven years in between having children. At that time, as soon as the foreman found out you were pregnant, they suspended you and you could not go back until after the baby was born. There was no maternity leave. While you were out, you were broke.

I went back to work for another year but became pregnant with our second child and had to leave for the duration of the pregnancy. Leroy and I stayed married for a few years. As I look back, I can see that it was foolishness that caused us to separate. One day I told Leroy that there were so many bed bugs in the bed that were biting our sons and I was going to spray the bed down real good the next day. Well, upon arising the next day, I did just that. But in the process, I found a bottle full of hair, which looked like mine. I became concerned and I went upstairs to his aunt and asked her if she knew what this bottle of hair meant and why it would be under our bed. She said she had no idea. I then went downstairs to my aunt and asked the same question. My aunt told me to give the bottle of hair to her. She sent it to my mom, who was still in the country (White Hall, SC). When my mom got that bottle of hair, she took it to a "root doctor" in Beaufort, SC. My mom said when the "root doctor" opened the bottle all the hair immediately flew away. I did not understand all of that but the next thing I knew my mom came to our apartment in Charleston, stood at the bottom of the stairs, and commanded me to pack my bags and move out. Apparently, my mom felt that whatever was in that bottle was meant to hurt me. She felt that my husband had to have cut some of my hair while I was asleep and placed it in that bottle.

I was in a big dilemma. I really did not want to leave my husband, but my mom was commanding me to do so. If I knew then, what I know now, I would have stayed with my husband. But, instead, I was obedient to my mom. I thought if I did not listen to her, she would be mad at me and I would not have anyone. So, I moved out.

Every day, when I was coming home from work or church, I would see Leroy and he would ask me when I was coming back home with him. In my heart, I wanted to go but was afraid that my mom would not be pleased if I did. I believed that I needed my mom, especially to help me with my boys because Leroy was always without a job.

After a while, Leroy got tired of asking me to return. Instead, he decided to move to New York. He told me, once he got settled, he would send for me. Well, time passed and I had not received tickets for the boys and me to go. Then, one day his brother was in town and came by to see me. I asked him if Leroy told him to bring me back to New York with him. He said, "No." I was torn between being unhappy and happy. I remember writing to a lady minister who came on the radio on Sundays. I explained my situation to her and asked her if she thought I should leave Charleston and go to New York to be with my husband. She read the response to my letter over the radio and said, if it were her, she would stay where she was. To me, that was confirmation that I was to stay in Charleston. Leroy never sent for me, and I never went. That was the end of our relationship. He would send money to the boys every now and then but no real support. We became estranged.

As time went on, I re-engaged in a previous relationship and became pregnant. That relationship did not last. Since my last name was still Bennett at the time, my youngest son took on this last name too. Because I had to work and had no one to take care of my three boys, my mom took them with her to White Hall. I would visit them on the weekends and take money and supplies to help support them. Well, a few years later, my mom's house caught fire and burned down. She could no longer keep all three boys. I also worked part time in a grocery store for Mrs. Brown. When she heard of the misfortune, she offered to take me to White Hall to check up on my mom and the boys. While there, she suggested that I let her take the youngest boy to live with her in North Charleston for a while, until our situation got better. In the meantime, my mom was able to find a place for her and the two older boys in White Hall.

My younger son was readily accepted into Mrs. Brown's family. As a matter of fact, when they registered him to start school, they registered him with their last name. Although I was not so comfortable with this, I found a way to accept it, since my maiden name was Brown. I looked at this as a blessing. The Brown's took really good care of my son. I would go to visit him on weekends and would take him to the country to spend time with his two older brothers. I wanted to ensure that my children all knew each other.

Then the unthinkable happened. I went to visit my son one weekend and the Browns did not want me to see him. They felt it would be better if he just stayed with them all of the time. At this point I became very disturbed. It seemed they were no longer just trying to help but wanted to actually take my son away from me. I tried to enter the porch to go to see my son and Mr. Brown pushed me off the porch and told me I could not come in. I went back to Charleston and got the man I thought of as my dad (Henry Brown, who was really my mom's oldest son). He returned with me to North Charleston and demanded that the Browns allow me to see my son.

He told them they had better not ever lay another hand on me. I took my son away from them and took him to the country to be reunited with his brothers.

Well, a tug of war began. The Browns would go to White Hall and take my son. Then my dad and I would go to their place and take him back. This back and forth continued for a while until one day I heard the biblical story about the two women who birthed babies. One woman's baby died and the other woman's baby lived. However, both women claimed the living baby as theirs. So the wise king decided he would cut the baby in half and give each mother a part. Based upon my misinterpretation, it appeared to me that the real mother could not bear the thought of her baby being cut in half, so she gave in and allowed the other woman to keep the baby. After much thought, I allowed the Browns to keep my son because they were in a much better position to take care of him. He always knew I was his mother and I tried to ensure he knew his brothers. I must say, the Browns did an excellent job with him. He was the valedictorian of his high school class and got a football scholarship, which helped to pay for his college education.

My older boys went into the U.S. Armed Services: One to the Army and one to the Marine Corps. As time passed, I met Elijah Floyd, who became my second husband. We had two sons. Elijah was a gambler and when he worked, he did not bring his money home. Instead, he would hang out with the boys and gamble. This caused problems between us and we eventually separated. He moved to Baltimore. After he was gone for a few years, I met someone else and became pregnant with my daughter. When Elijah found out, he agreed to adopt our daughter and asked us to come to Baltimore to live. We packed our bags and off to Baltimore we went.

This proved to be a challenging time for me. I was unable to find any work. The only thing I really knew how to do was make cigars.

Elijah had a job, but he wasn't making much money and he still gambled. I can remember not having enough milk to make a bottle for my baby girl. Elijah was able to find enough change to get a can of cream. After much looking, I was able to find a job sitting with a sick lady. I did not even have a decent pair of shoes. So with my first pay check, I bought a pair of shoes. That same day, it rained so hard that by the time I got home, the shoes had torn apart. I was at a low point and after much thought, I decided to leave Baltimore with my three children and go back home to Charleston, where I had a better chance of finding work.

Upon my return, I was able to get a job at the Cigar Factory in the day and the Cavalier Restaurant at night. By now, my mom had passed and I had no help with my children. Because I needed to work and did not want them home alone, I found good people to watch over my children. My grand aunt looked after the two boys and my friend Alice looked after my one girl. Again, I was blessed to have people who actually loved my children and provided excellent care.

My grand aunt became in poor health and passed away. I then brought my boys to live with me. By then, they were old enough to be home alone. My daughter remained with Alice. I would pick her up late every night when I got off from the Cavalier Restaurant. Finally, Alice suggested that because of my hours, I should just let the baby stay with her and visit every day. I found this to be a workable arrangement. This went on until my daughter was about six or seven years old. However, it got to a point where the environment at Alice's house changed. She started having all types of strange people hanging out at her house. I also found that my daughter was picking up bad habits from this environment. I made the hard decision to take my daughter away from Alice. This really hurt her and she begged me to reconsider, but I had made up my mind that I could not allow my daughter to be in an inappropriate environment. Alice vowed she would put those people out and clean up her situation, but I stood firm in my decision. After Alice did what she said and got rid of the people who were living in her house, I then allowed my daughter to go there for after-school care only. She would come home every day with me and her two brothers. By the time she was about nine years old, we moved to the projects, which were in another part of town. My eldest son was then able to be responsible for them until I got off from work.

We lived in the projects for a couple of years. The problem was whenever I got a raise on my job, the rent would go up. It got to the point where it was not cost effective to live in the projects. We moved to a place that I could better afford. It was on Nassau Street. My childhood friend Louise and her husband owned this property, which had a two level house in the backyard. We lived upstairs and another family lived downstairs.

Eventually, the Cigar Factory began experiencing financial problems and I was laid off. After all the combined twenty seven years of working there, I received no compensation. All I got was a pink slip saying they had to let me go. I decided to go back to school at night and get my high school diploma. I was successful and that achievement opened up a few new doors for me. I got a job as a cashier at the TG&Y store and did that for a few years.

By now, my older son Junior had graduated high school and gone into the Army. My younger son did not finish high school but decided to try the Job Corps. That did not work for him, so he returned home and found work. My daughter had now graduated high school and was attending college. She was always smart and motivated to do well in life. She was able to get scholarships, grants, and loans to pay for her college education. I did not know how to advise her and no one that I knew tried to help. But, thanks be to God, she had teachers and counselors, who saw her potential and provided guidance and direction.

Now it is just my youngest son and me in the house. I took a nursing course but before I began my studies I worked for a doctor and his wife earning $1.50 an hour to care for their child four hours a day. Then I left there and went into the school system, at Charleston High School, as a maid. When that school closed down, I went to Burke High School to work as a custodian.

While my daughter was in college, she joined the Reserve Officer Training Corps (ROTC). By the time she reached her junior year, she was getting a stipend of $100 per month. She encouraged me to look for a Title IX House. I began saving as much as I could for a down payment. With a lot of prayer and a little bit of money, I was able to bid on a town house and won the bid. This was a happy day for us all. We had never owned a house. My daughter sent her ROTC check to me each month to help out and my son and I did our part to keep this home. After my daughter graduated from college, she was commissioned into the Army as a second lieutenant. One of the first things she did was make out an allotment to me that paid the house note and helped with other bills.

Even after she got married, she continued to help me financially. Her husband has always been there for her and me. When they had their first and only child, I was there for them, as they had been for me. This was the only grand that I actually witnessed come into this world. Whenever my daughter needed me to help out, I would go. She and her husband would take care of all my bills and expenses while I was with them, which allowed me to be able to up and go at will. I spent time with them in Atlanta after my granddaughter was born. I spent time with them in Indianapolis while they were in school for the military. I spent time with them in Texas when they had summer camp for the Army. I then moved to Germany to care for my granddaughter while they had challenging assignments. I lived with them in Kansas and cared for my granddaughter. I lived with them in North Carolina. Of course by then my granddaughter was getting to be a teenager and did not require as much care. But this was a time of enjoyment for me. While in North Carolina, I moved into my own apartment, which was about ten minutes away from them. We saw each other almost every day and they picked me up for church and other activities. I got a little job as a greeter at the Harris Teeter Grocery Store. I had friends my age in the apartment complex. It was a nice experience.

My second oldest son and his wife asked me to come back to Charleston to help out with my grandson. My daughter-in-law was a nurse and worked the late shift; and my son's job required a long-distance daily commute. I agreed to do this and moved back to Charleston in 1999. I was able to buy a house that was just down the street from them.

I went back to North Carolina to see my granddaughter graduate from high school. This was a proud day for all of us. I also went with her and her parents when she moved into her dormitory at the University of North Carolina at Chapel Hill (UNC-Chapel Hill). This was another proud day for us. God even blessed me to go to her graduation from UNC-Chapel Hill in 2004. She is in the television broadcasting field and has worked several jobs. Some of those jobs included being an anchor/reporter with CBS in Shreveport, LA and a reporter/anchor with CBS in Miami.

I went back to Charleston and continued to help with my grandson. As he got older, he did not need as much care. I spent much time with my church and I started working at the after-school center as a "grandmother" figure. I did this for a few years, but my age caught up with me and lessened my ability to do the things I used to do. I know that getting old is a blessing, but it sure can be inconvenient sometimes.

My daughter and son-in-law saw how my health was failing and offered to let me come and live with them. I am so grateful that God laid it on their hearts and minds to do so. My son-in-law is more like a son. He works from home and he is really my primary caregiver during the day. I know that I am old and forgetful. I know that I sometimes sound like a broken record because I may ask the same questions over and over again. I always let them know that my brain just don't hold on to things and to please forgive me if I repeat myself so much. I can honestly say that God is going to bless these two people beyond measure. They have taken me in and they continue to love me and care for me and give me my flowers while I am living.

I call my son-in-law my baby boy because he is the youngest of all my sons. I see him as a son and not a son-in-law. He takes care of me like a baby. He ensures I get a hot breakfast every morning and that I take my medicines. He is the one who takes me to my medical appointments. My daughter works in Washington, DC, but when she comes home, she and I eat dinner together almost every night. She and I spend time together on the weekends. Sometimes we go to Walmart, the grocery store or out for ice cream. Because we live in Virginia and she works in DC, her commute is almost two hours one way, which equates to almost a total of 4 hours each day. That's almost like a part-time job. I am currently eighty nine years old and I am truly blessed. I can honestly say that my daughter and my "baby boy" continue to be a godsend in my life.

I know what they are going through because I took care of two mothers. When my adopted mother and my birth mother were sick at the same time, I knew I could not care for both of them. So I took care of Susan, my adopted mother, until she died. Then I took care of Hattie, my birth mother, until she died. I even ended up taking care of Hattie's husband, until he died.

Thank God I have a great, godly son-in-law and a precious daughter. They don't let me need for anything. I also have five sons. A couple of them help out sometimes. Although I had a hard time raising my children, God brought us out to this day. I didn't have great husbands, but I had Jesus and I still have Him. I can smile happily because Jesus is my best friend. He picked me up and He turned me around. He planted my feet on higher ground. I have served God since I was five years old. I was in the world but not of the world. I never danced, drank beer, wine, or whiskey. I did go to parties, but I was the designated "sober one" in the group. I took care of friends' pocketbooks while they had their fun. Most of my activities involved church work until now. And I am so glad because I had to be mom and dad for my children. I could not afford to develop expensive habits. My life was tough, but I always had God in it and by His grace and mercy, I always will.

I truly believe the Lord is blessing me right now. I cared for others when they needed me. And now the Lord has sent my daughter and my "baby boy" to care for me in my time of need. I am so happy and I am so blessed.

CHAPTER 2

A Taste of Gullah

Charleston, South Carolina is known as the "low country," "the Peninsula City," and also "the City by the Sea." It is known as one of the places where the language of Gullah is spoken and the people refer to themselves as "Geechees." Well, I am a Geechee and people often tell me I sound like I am West Indian, Bahamian, Jamaican, or from one of the Caribbean Islands.

We Geechees tend to get a little excited, at times, when we speak. We may leave out a helping verb or two or three. For example, instead of saying "I am going to the store and I will see you in a while, we may say "I gwoing to da sto—I see you assawhile." Now, depending on how good your listening and interpretation skills are, you may have thought I just cursed (but, I didn't).

To give you an historical perspective, the Gullah people are Black folks who live in the low country region of South Carolina and Georgia. This includes both the coastal plain and the Sea Islands. The region used to extend to North Carolina and Florida, but now the area is confined to the South Carolina and Georgia Low Country.

I will give you a chance to see how well you can read and/or speak my language. Below is a typical conversation that you might hear between me and one of my friends or between other Geechees.

By Golly Cholly, de man done gone way down da street. U say whey he been at and why he da run way so fast? Cum da fine out, he done teaf from da Walmart and now he tryin ta-git wey. But da policeman, he chase um down and he catch um. Den he jack um up gainst da car. Den da policeman he pull out de club an he stad de beat um down. Yeah he beat um down bad. All da people who see dat say, why da policeman beat um down so bad and somebody say, da policeman beat um down cause he teaf da stuff from da sto and try da run wey on foot.

Translation:

A man stole something from Walmart and ran away real fast. The policeman chased him and caught him. Then the policeman pushed him against the car, pulled out his club, and started to beat him. The people who saw this wondered why the policeman beat the man so badly. Somebody said, "The policeman beat him so badly because he stole from the store and tried to get away."

My daughter looked up the meaning of Geechee on the Internet. There were several definitions, but the one I will focus on is the one that says the Gullah people and their language are called Geechees. It further stated that the term Geechee was a cultural term used by those who speak the language and "Gullah" was a term generally used by outsiders. It has become sort of a code for speakers to formally identify themselves and their language.

It is said that many scholars believe Gullah came about in South Carolina and Georgia in the 18th and 19th centuries when African slaves on rice plantations made up their own Creole language. They combined parts of English they learned in America with the West and Central African languages they brought with them on the Middle Passage.

According to this view, Gullah is an independent language developed in North America. Scholars maintain that some of the slaves brought to South Carolina and Georgia already knew West African Pidgin English before they left Africa, as it was spoken along the West African coast during the 18th century as a language of trade between Europeans and Africans and between Africans of different tribes.

Lorenzo Dow Turner, an African American linguist, is known as the "Father of Gullah Studies." His research revealed that Gullah is a strongly influenced African language with its sound system, vocabulary, grammar, sentence structure, and semantic organization. Before his work, mainstream scholars viewed Gullah as sub-standard English, a hodgepodge of mispronounced words and corrupted grammar, which uneducated Black people developed in their efforts to copy the speech of their English, Irish, Scottish, and French slave owners.

For generations, people who spoke Gullah were stigmatized. Their language was thought of as a mark of ignorance and given low social status. As a result, Gullah people developed the habit of speaking their language only in the confines of their homes and local communities.

In doing an Internet search on Gullah my daughter discovered that United States Supreme Court Justice Clarence Thomas was raised as a Gullah speaker in coastal Georgia. It was noted that when asked why he has little to say during hearings of the court, he responded that in his early years he was ridiculed for speaking Gullah. As a defensive mechanism he developed the habit of listening, rather than speaking in public.

The Gullah people speak a Creole language similar to Sierra Leone Krio. They use African names, tell African folktales, make African-style handicrafts, such as baskets and carved walking sticks. If you visit the beautiful and historic city of Charleston, you must go downtown and walk through the Market, where slaves were once auctioned and partake of the delicious Gullah cuisine.

As a matter of fact, the Geechees enjoy a rich cuisine, which includes a lot of rice dishes. I can remember eating rice every day and in almost every way. In the movie Forrest Gump, Bubba knew his shrimp and he said, "Shrimp is the fruit of the sea." Well the Gullah people really know their rice and we think, "Rice is the starch of the land." There is white rice, brown rice, yellow rice, and red rice; there is rice and greens, rice and okra, rice and gravy; there is rice-a-roni, rice pilaf, and rice casserole. You put rice in gumbo and you put rice in soup. You make rice and corn and you make hop-n-johns, which is a form of rice and field peas, which we eat on New Year's Day. We eat rice for breakfast, as a cereal with milk and we also eat rice cakes. So you see Bubba and Forrest ain't got nothing on us.

Rice was something that led to forming a special link between the Gullah people and the people of Sierra Leone. The Middle Passage bears witness to the connection that began as slaves were brought to America to promote the cultivation of rice on the plantations and to enrich the agricultural-based economy of that time. But rice is not the only thing the Gullah people are known for. They have other customs and traditions that involve arts and crafts, storytelling, music and dance, as well as worship and burial customs. In recent years, educated Gullah people have begun promoting the use of their language as a symbol of cultural pride.

There is a Charleston Club in the DC/Maryland/Virginia area that sponsors a social each year featuring, "A Taste of Gullah." They put together a beautiful event that honors our culture. One year, there was a female comedian, who did an excellent job of storytelling and making jokes about the Gullah people and their ways. In 2014, Gil was asked to be the keynote speaker. You see, he was well qualified, as I taught him the Gullah ways very well. He gave an excellent presentation on the importance of mentoring, especially our African American males and standing our ground. Afterwards, there was a Gullah Contest. Each table had someone to tell a story or a joke in Gullah. Everyone in the place was laughing so hard that tears were flowing everywhere—that is, tears of joy. This annual activity is a great way to keep the Gullah culture alive and show appreciation for our part in history that continues to this day.

CHAPTER 3

Lucille-Isms

In Lucille's Voice

The previous chapter gave you a taste of Gullah. Well, there are many sayings that I constantly use, which my children call Lucille-isms. I am not sure who created them but they were sayings that were passed along during my upbringing. Some of them have stories behind them and others don't. Hopefully you will enjoy this section and maybe even find some humor in some of them.

#1) "Fo good vittles waste . . . belly bust."

I was brought up in an environment where waste was not an option. Food was hard to come by and you were expected to eat every drop on your plate. It is amazing how your upbringing can stick with you for life. For some people, it is easy to rise above the poor mentality. For others, it is a little more difficult. I am one who likes to stick with the old ways. Although I am much better off today than I have ever been, I still eat every drop that is placed on my plate. I often say people may think I have not had enough to eat because of the way I eat. You can bet my plate will be clean when I have finished a meal. Even if I am full, I refuse to throw food away. I will store it and continually go back to it until it is all gone. I strongly believe before good food wastes, I will eat until my stomach can hold no more. In the Gullah language: "Fo good vittles waste, belly bust."

To make it even clearer, we Geechees love to tell stories. This one happens to be true. One morning I made breakfast and I asked my children, "Who wants grits?" Three of them said they did. Since there was not much, I gave it all to them and I had none. After I put the grits on one of the boys' plate, he decided he did not want them. I left out of the kitchen for a while and when I returned, I stepped on the porch to place something into the big garbage can. To my surprise, I saw the grits in the trash. Immediately I asked the boys if they all ate their grits and they all said, "Yes." I went on to say I saw my grits in the trash and demanded to know who put them there. When my son admitted to doing this I took him by the hand, made him get a plate, and had him to follow me outside to the garbage. I stood over him and made him use his fingers to scoop up all of my grits out of that can and I made him eat every drop. You can imagine that to this day, he hates grits. In today's society that might be considered as child abuse. But the moral of the story was, "Food was too hard to come by in my house and it would not be wasted." The other lesson learned was that lying was an unacceptable practice in my house and there were consequences for such actions.

#2) "Once a woman—twice a child."

If you live long enough, you may find that you sometimes revert to childish ways. At almost 90 years old, I realize that I need my children more than I ever have. As a matter of fact, I am currently a dependent of my daughter and her husband. In essence, they are now responsible for me. Just like a child, they ensure all of my needs are met and most of my wants. This includes my physical needs (food, clothing, housing, and medicines); my financial needs (bills paid, church tithes and offerings paid, as well as spending change); social and emotional needs (taking me to social activities, senior citizen classes, shopping, and other outings); and spiritual needs (taking me to church activities, praying together, and engaging in spiritual conversations). They even try to provide most of the things that I want, but I try not to want for much.

Just as children are dependent upon their parents, senior citizens are sometimes dependent upon their children, especially as we age and our memory starts to fade and our bodies start to slow down. For some, it can be a sad and depressing time. For others, it is just another stage of life. However, I have found that if I focus on the things for which I am thankful, I can self—motivate through the frustrations of aging.

When I do get into a rut because of losing much of my independence, it is nice to have a wonderful daughter and her husband around to encourage me. A few years ago, when I first moved in with my daughter and her husband, I was home alone and decided to cook something. To make a long story short, I forgot about the pot and it burned so badly that smoke was everywhere. The smoke alarm went off and I was very frightened. I turned on the stove's fan and opened the kitchen door, then called my daughter. Her first question was, "Are you alright?" Then she asked a few more questions to determine if she needed to come home. After speaking to her, I felt much better. She told me what to do to start airing out the house. When she came home, the house still smelled a little smoky but she took over and got things back to normal. We had a family discussion and all decided that I was not to use the stove when home alone. However, I could use the microwave. Just as children are prohibited from certain things, so are seniors as we age. We have to give up certain things that affect our safety and the safety of others.

#3) "Only fly in the milk."

This saying has racial overtones. It refers to the only African American among other ethnic groups that have lighter skin or the person in the room with the darkest complexion. An example would be someone saying, "President Barack Obama is the only fly in the milk among other American Commanders-In-Chief." Another example would be someone saying, "In her class, she was the only fly in the milk." Normally, this kind of conversation is held among African Americans about African Americans, and it is acceptable. However, if someone from another ethnic group said the same thing, it could be considered negative, derogatory, or even racist.

#4) "They don't care more 'bout me than crow care 'bout Sunday."

This saying focuses on a fact that when the farmer plants his or her corn, the crow will come and eat it no matter what day of the week it is. The crow seems to only be concerned about its own wellbeing. When it travels in a flock, it is concerned only about those in that flock. The analogy is that at times, people do the same thing. They don't care about anyone or anything, except themselves or those in their immediate sight. For me, it is not such a good feeling to know that some of my family and friends, to whom I have shown love and care, don't seem to have the time, energy, or resources to reciprocate. In essence, they don't care anymore about me than a crow cares about Sunday. However, I always have to remember these powerful two words—but God. Yes, God loves me. God cares for me. God provides for me. He always sends His angels to do His good work. And for that, I am thankful.

#5) "Belly full, behind glad."

I think all of us have experienced this. It may be after breakfast, lunch, or dinner but once you have eaten a nice, sizeable meal you start to feel sleepy and want to lay down for a nap. This is when your belly is full and your behind is glad.

#6) "He don't take no tea for the fever."

There are people who can endure much pain and they do not like to take medicine, even when they are sick. They find other methods for relief that do not involve using medicine. In other words, they don't take no tea for the fever.

#7) "You are a crane with one gut."

Back in my day old folks could tell when a young girl or woman was pregnant. They would describe you as a crane with one gut.

#8) "Wherever you be, let your wind go free, 'cause that was the death of poor Rosalie."

It is a biological function to release gas. However, it is not looked upon as one of the most courteous things to do, especially in public. There is an old folks' tale about a person named Rosalie, who held her gas so often that it led to her death. Thus came the saying, "Wherever you be, let your wind run free, 'cause that was the death of poor Rosalie."

#9) "The mouth that was made to eat bread shall not eat grass."

There is a gospel song by recording artist Yolanda Adams that says, "What God has for me is for me." As we define our purpose in this life, we begin to understand that those of us who have a Divine calling on our lives are meant to fulfill our specific destinies. In many cases, we have gifts that are yet to be discovered but what is meant to be will be because our mouths that were made to eat bread shall not eat grass instead.

#10) "Where there is no fool, there is no fun."

In every group there is usually a person who clowns around or acts like a fool. In many cases, he or she is seen as the life of the party. In the classroom, there is the class clown who keeps everybody laughing. At the comic show, there is the comedian who brings comic relief. The point is that laughter is medicine for the soul and people who clown around add to the fun. Therefore, "Where there is no fool there is no fun."

#11) "It ain't about what you drive, it's about what you drive up to. Or is it?"

The Lucille-ism listed above is followed by a question because the answer depends on your perspective. Many of us desire the better things in life, such as nice homes, nice cars, and money in our pockets. However, many people cannot afford to acquire these things all at once.

Just because you are poor does not mean you don't like nice things and want them. So, go ahead and save for a pair of expensive tennis shoes or a flat screen television or even a car because that amount of money is reachable in a reasonably short time. Being able to have something nice makes one feel good. Just make sure that the things for which you save are worth having.

#12) "A hard head makes a soft behind."

In my day, it was nothing to paddle or spank a child for misbehaving. It was a part of training up a child in the right way. If your parents told you to do something, you did it. The same was true for your teacher, or any other respectable adult. You were not allowed to grumble or be disrespectful in any way. If you chose to be disobedient, then you felt the rod. In essence, your hard head caused you to get a spanking.

#13) "A stomach full ain't but a stomach full."

As long as you get to eat some kind of food, whether it is rich and nutritious or poor and fatty, what matters in the end is that you are not hungry.

#14) "If the Woodpecker wants sweet meat, he got to stand some pecking in the head."

Sometimes people say and do mean things to you. People may nag and taunt you. However, if you want to experience joy and happiness, you sometimes have to go through unpleasant stuff.

#15) "They won't give you a whoop in hell if you lost."

Sometimes people can be uncaring. You can be down and out, you can be hungry. You can be on your last dime and people will show no mercy, sympathy, or empathy. People may see you are lost, but they won't help you to be found. You can stay there and burn up as far as they are concerned. The truth is, they are scared that you might be rescued and do better than them.

#16) "Gone out like high top button shoes."

Obsolete, out of style, or old fashioned.

#17) "'I see,' said the blind man."

In most cases, if you are considered to be blind you cannot see. Therefore, when the blind man can see something, it means that it is so simple, so transparent that even someone with challenges understands.

#18) "He don't think like man."

Supposedly, a man should be the epitome of strength. When he falls short it is believed that he is not mature in his thought process. Therefore, he is seen as a childish or immature man.

#19) "Any him da him."

Whatever you say is alright with me. I am not choosy. I am flexible.

#20) "Every dog got e day and every cat got e afternoon."

This means what goes around comes around. What you do to others can come back to you.

#21) "Rabbit don't stray far from the bush."

If you were trained a certain way, you won't go astray—at least not for long.

#22) "A heap see, but a few know."

Many people may see a situation but unless they walk in the shoes of those involved, they really don't understand.

Carolyn Evaughn Knowles

#23) "Hold your mule."

It's inappropriate to let out gas when in close quarters. That's when you and/or someone else may pray that you "hold your mule."

#24) "The ole gray mule ain't what it used to be."

As the years pass and we become senior citizens, we find that we can't do the things we used to be able to do. Getting old is a blessing.

CHAPTER 4

Aging with Dignity in Granny Shoes

(Explained by Carolyn)

In the fall of 2010, Gil and I made a major decision that would change our lives forever. We realized that my mom had been on a decline for a few years and she had hinted many times about coming to live with us again. You see, she had lived with us before for nearly 12 years. She played a major role in the upbringing of our one and only daughter. I can remember when we were stationed in Zweibrucken, Germany, I served as a company commander of a data processing unit. Gil commuted daily to Pirmasens, which was about 30-45 minutes away. As commander, I was responsible for over 200 soldiers, civilian workers, and German nationals. It was nothing for me to be put on alert in the wee hours of the morning. This is when we had to get into full MOPP 4 gear that protected us from chemical, biological, radiological, and nuclear attacks and practice for war. Whenever this happened, we had to take our four-year-old daughter to our neighbors' (Jo and Ham) house. Jo was the director of the child care center. She would prepare Summer for day care and take her there for us. As the drills were usually over by 8:00 a.m., I could then go by the center to check on our baby girl.

I can remember telling my mom these stories of morning alerts and having to drag Summer out of bed and taking her to a friend's home, so we could fulfill our military duties. Well, this did not go over well with my mom. She indicated she did not like her granddaughter being dragged out of bed so often and taken to another household for care.

In the military we had to have a non-combatant plan when deployed overseas, which meant someone had to be designated to take care of our dependents should the environment become hostile and there was a need to send noncombatants home. Mom indicated she wanted to come to Germany to take care of her granddaughter. Her decision had a great impact on me. She was willing to give up her life in South Carolina to come to a foreign country and help our family.

We began to make plans for mom's arrival. Gil helped her to get a passport for an extended period. Mom quit her job as a custodian at one of the local high schools. She informed them that her daughter needed her.

It was arrival day at the Frankfurt Airport. Gil went to meet my mom. To hear him tell this story is hilarious. I often mentioned to my mom that we missed eating things like fresh collard greens, okra, and other vegetables. Well, Gil said when he picked her up at the airport her luggage was dripping. It appeared my mom brought frozen vegetables in her suitcase, which had thawed out during the 9 1/2 – hour flight. He said she had rope tied around the suitcases because they were old. She had on a little "mammy-made" skirt with tennis shoes. Picture this: a little old lady in tennis shoes with dripping suitcases, tied with rope, about to start a new chapter in her life, as well as ours. Gil said one of the first things he did was stop along the way and purchase new luggage for my mom.

Mom stayed with us for two of the three years we spent in Germany. She was a godsend. We had a little "bourgeois" dog named Humphrey. Mom had never dealt with any kind of pet before. However, she and Humphrey became good friends. As a matter of fact, because they were together all day, I think they became great friends. She walked, fed, and played with him. He loved her and she loved him.

While in Germany, mom cared for Summer and also became known as the grandmother of the three-story building, where we lived, which was referred to as the "Stairwells." Whenever one of the children could not go to school because of minor illness, mom would care for them. By the time we left Germany, mom was celebrated with more farewell parties than I was. She was feted by the stairwell community, our church, and the Zweibrucken Arts and Crafts Community Center, where she spent much of her free time.

After we left Germany mom moved to Kansas with us, still providing care and support to our family. When we were reassigned to North Carolina, mom moved with us again. By then, our daughter was a pre-teen and was becoming very independent. However, mom remained an active part of our family. She wanted to get an apartment of her own that was in close proximity to us. We found her a place that was about ten minutes away. We saw her practically every day and picked her up for all church activities. She established some friendships with other seniors in her apartment complex and enjoyed her new space.

One of my brothers and his wife asked her to move back to South Carolina to help with their son. She agreed and that's why she returned to South Carolina. For several years, things were fine. She was still very independent and very active. She visited us every summer and spent holidays with us. As my nephew became older, he became more independent. Mom was also getting older and beginning to feel less valued. She began volunteering at an after-school center. That worked well for a while. But then she began to complain about how rude the children were. She would also walk to the center to work every day, causing constant pain in her legs. I would send money for her to take taxis to and from work, but she refused, saying that the taxis were too expensive.

My brother was able to enroll her in the city's tele-ride program, which worked for a while. Eventually, the situation grew unworkable. Mom often commented on how untimely the service was. They would pick her up too early and she would arrive at work sometimes an hour before her start time or they would pick her up too late, sometimes an hour or so after her quitting time. The work at the center began to wear mom down, but she did not want to quit. I believe she viewed it as a social outlet. But, it appeared all she did was talk about how terribly rude the children were and how her legs hurt all the time.

Finally, my brother and I convinced her it was time to quit. She was 84 years old. The problem then became her being alone all day and night. She often said the telephone was her company. I would feel so terrible every time I spoke with her because she said that no one visited her and she didn't get out of the house, except on Sundays and Wednesdays for church and bible study. For some, the slower schedule would seem like a good thing. However, mom had always been active and independent, so she hated the inactivity. Another year passed and mom was now 85. She indicated many times how she would like to move back in with us. I was not ready to do this because we lived in Virginia and Gil and I worked a far distance from where we lived. My commute was 1 ½—2 hours one way. If something was to happen to her, it would take me too long to get home. When mom turned 86, my brothers and I gave her a birthday party. More than 100 family members and friends attended. Just before her birthday, Gil and I discussed how we noticed the decline of her physical, emotional, and spiritual health. He had started a home-based business, which made it easier for us to decide that it was time to ask her if she wanted to move back in with us. She was elated and immediately said, "Yes." Her birthday party was in September. We agreed that when she came to us after Thanksgiving, it would be her effective change of residence. In November 2010, we drove to South Carolina for Thanksgiving and brought mom back to Virginia. It was understood that mom could visit, especially during the summers and holidays. She would always have a place to go.

Of course things don't always go as planned. The house had to be rented and therefore, a new level of drama began for mom. Instead of always having a place to return, we were now telling her she needed to completely move out of the house so that it could be rented. Mom went back to South Carolina for a month to go through her things and found it very difficult to part with her stuff. She said they were her lifelong belongings. She wanted to have yard sales and did so, but there were not many buyers. There were not even many onlookers. What was valuable to her was not valuable to others. Mom began to sink into a depression that started a downward spiral.

After a month, mom's roundtrip airline ticket was due to return her to us. She came back to Virginia, but her whole conversation focused on her "stuff." Once again we reacted. We told her that she would have another opportunity to go back in August when we went on vacation. We decided to buy a one-way ticket and purchase her return flight ticket when she was ready to come back. She found this to be agreeable. We decided that after our vacation, I would go to South Carolina to help her finalize the move. Her doctor agreed we needed to close that chapter so that she could start anew.

Gil re-enrolled mom in senior day care. She was to begin upon her return to Virginia. Prior to going to South Carolina this last time mom was sick for about a month. She constantly talked about the pain in her legs and hips; the numbness of her fingers and toes, the closing of one eye lid and the fogginess in the other. It seemed like it was just so much. Gil and I were beginning to be overwhelmed; especially him, since by default he was her primary caregiver. We thought bringing mom to Virginia would be good for her. She was not alone. She had us to care for and support her. She would go with us to church and other social activities. But, she continued to constantly mention her pains. We went to mom's doctor with these issues. She prescribed a stronger pain medicine. However, mom had a bad reaction to the medicine (dizziness and vomiting). We returned to the doctor. Mom was taken off that medicine and was placed on a narcotic patch. Again, this proved to be too strong. You see, she is only 4 feet 10 inches tall and weighs about 115 pounds. That's why we affectionately call her "Li'l Lady." She experienced continued vomiting, dizziness, and lethargy. We returned to the doctor and the dosage was lowered. However, the same reaction continued for about a month. She became a different person. All she did was sleep. She barely ate and became very dependent and feeble. After praying about it, Gil and I consulted with the doctor and decided to take her off the pain medication completely. The next step was pain management. After being off the medicine for about two weeks, she slowly started to become more active. She got out of bed, was not dizzy, and the vomiting ceased. We said, "Thank God." But, of course, the pain returned. At this point, we believed it was better to work with pain management while she was still mobile sans the dizziness or nauseous stomach.

Our decision seemed to work for a while, but then other aches and pains seemed prominent in mom's mind. And of course she had to verbalize all of them. We thought, "Wow, mom is in a beautiful, loving home. She has her own suite complete with a bedroom, dayroom, and full bath. She receives a hot breakfast and hot dinner every day, with snacks available throughout the day. However, she still finds something negative on which to focus." The ironic thing is that she does not seem to think she complains. As a matter of fact, she says there are people who complain all the time and that she is so glad she's not one of them.

Mom's typical response to people when they ask her a simple question like "How are you today" is, "I ain't doing all they say, but I'm here." Instead of responding, "Fine." I think that her answer is so negative for someone who is so blessed. I asked her one day why it is that she responds like that. She said people asked her and she's being honest. I asked her, "What do you mean by 'all they' say? Who are they?" She said, "People may say you look good, but that does not mean you feel good." The difference between my mom's mindset and mine is this: I choose to say I am fine even when I'm not. I don't see that as being dishonest, I see it as speaking power and blessings into my life.

I take a lot of time to ensure that mom is well kept and that she especially looks good when going out. I always try to look nice and want her to look nice too. When she receives compliments, she may say, "Thank you," but not without a dose of negativity. Her response would be more like "Thank you, but the looks don't tell you 'bout these aches and pains, 'cause I hurts all day and all night." My thoughts are that pretty soon, people may stop asking, "How are you today?" Gil and I came to the conclusion that when you see mom really happy and being positive, he and I are worn out! We are trying to honor and care for her even though it is very challenging. We know it is the right thing to do for such a time as this.

Mom is now in "Granny Shoes." She can no longer wear the high heels and stilettos that were once a part of her signature apparel. However, I must say, she is still cute in her granny shoes and beautiful hats . . . she wears them well. Gil and I get comfort in knowing that we are contributing to her "aging with dignity."

Part II

May's Flower

May's Flower

By
Carolyn Knowles

On a beautiful day in the month of May,
a mother gave yet another birth.
But this time while sighing, she heard the crying of
a baby girl delivered to this earth.

After having five boys whom she loved very much,
God sent her another blessing packaged as such.
To be born in the month of May at that appointed hour,
to her was yet another sign of God's great power.

The Lily of the Valley—May's Flower would be,
symbolizing beauty, fragrance, and humility.
May's Flower would bloom late in the spring,
and once it had sprung—what a beautiful thing.

Beauty on the inside and outside as well,
May's Flower is exquisite with a captivating smell.
Its unrivaled splendor makes it stand out,
as a gift to remember, without any doubt.

It exudes the four elements—earth, water, fire, and air;
it is exceedingly fruitful, while under the gardener's care.
It contended with the rose for queen,
in Solomon's kingdom of flowers,
but as the Lily of the Valley,
it also symbolizes nature's great power.

You must bloom where you are, to be a May Flower,
being modestly humble, yet having great power.
Just as Christ came into this world, lowly and meek,
He became our Savior—the One whom we must seek.

May's Flower lives among thorns but it grows and it thrives,
it adds beauty, fragrance, and humility to many, many lives.
So as May's Flower blooms in and fades away,
its legacy will live on with each passing day.

CHAPTER 5

Worn Out Shoes, Platforms, Combat Boots, and High Heels

I gave a speech at Toastmasters a few years ago highlighting their theme of the year, "Courage to Conquer." In my own life, I have had to find that courage. I was born to a single mom, who provided for my brothers and me as best she could. I have had to overcome many challenges in my personal, professional, and spiritual life. Not having a father in the home could have led to negative and promiscuous behavior, but that was not the case. Having a strong mother with strong moral and ethical values helped me to set boundaries at an early age. I was brought up in a Christian Methodist Episcopal Church, where I learned biblical principles that have stayed with me throughout my life. When problems arose, I knew how to call on the name of Jesus and receive an answer—although it may have been delayed, delivered, or even denied.

I don't recall anything extraordinary in my early childhood except, after completion of kindergarten, I was able to skip first grade and begin my elementary school years in second grade. This action meant I was usually younger than my peers. I think being with older kids forced me to mature earlier than usual.

Elementary school was a time of school hopping. I think this caused me to have worn out shoes at an early age. I can remember attending three different schools: Henry P. Archer for second and third grades; Mitchell for fourth grade; back to Henry P. Archer for fifth and sixth grades; and finally Courtney for seventh grade. In Charleston, we did not have middle schools. Elementary was first to seventh grades and high school was eighth to twelfth grades. So as you might surmise, I did not have a chance to establish and maintain strong, lasting friendships. My shoes seemed to be worn out in my early years from so many moves.

A big part of my life was molded by Alice, who was mentioned earlier in the book. When I was in fourth grade, my family moved to the west side of town. My youngest brother was five years older than me. Therefore, we were able to stay home by ourselves. Alice and I visited every day. When I was in fifth grade, we moved to the projects, which placed us back on the east side. We lived there for two years and then in seventh grade, we moved again—to Nassau Street, which was also on the east side of town.

I began my eighth grade year at Charles A. Brown High School. This was a more stable period for me. I became friends with a group of girls that continued throughout my high school years and in some cases through college. Alice moved to a house that was right across the street from my school. She was known as the crazy lady, who worked in the corner grocery store. She was definitely my advocate. She did not want anyone to lay a hand on me, not even my mother. I can recall times when I misbehaved and Alice would step in for me so that my mom would not spank me. I can also remember in high school when a girl wanted to fight me because she claimed I took her boyfriend. The word was out that she and her friends were planning to jump me after school. Well, I called Alice and told her about it. To those girls' surprise, Alice met me at the school and confronted them asking, "Where are the bitches, who want to fight

Carolyn Floyd? If you want to fight, come on and fight me. I've got something for you and you can bring your mama too." You should have seen those girls run. This was just one of the many instances where Alice showed an unwavering love for me.

I can also remember how my mom made most of my clothes because she could not afford to buy them. But Alice had a charge account at Lerner's, a ladies clothing store. She would allow me to get anything I wanted. She always said, "Baby can get anything I've got." And that was absolutely true. Please don't think this love was one-sided because I had an unwavering love for Alice. I can remember throughout my high school days, I would stop by Alice's house every day to spend time with her and to run errands for her. When I went off to college, I wrote her often and she sent care packages and spending change. Whenever I returned home, Alice was always a part of my every day rounds. Alice was there for many of the special events in my life, whether in person or in thought. I felt her love at my graduations, wedding, Summer's birth and christening. Alice passed away in her late eighties. I will always have loving memories of this giant in my life. She helped me to develop into the woman I am today.

Of all the places I lived as a child, the one that stands out most in my mind is the house on Nassau Street. I refer to it as a back yard house, which means the landlord lived in the big front house, located on the street and renters lived in the two-story house, located in the back yard. The two stories were separated by an external staircase. My family lived on the second floor.

As I mentioned earlier, prior to moving on Nassau Street, we lived in the projects. And, believe it or not, I liked the projects. I thought of them as a nice place to live and play. They were relatively new and made of brick. I had friends who lived close by and we were happy there until we could no longer afford the rent. Our new residence on Nassau Street was quite different. It was very old and in need of repair. I was about 12 years old at the time and really started to notice how poor we were. I became more cognizant of the way I looked and the way my family lived, as compared to others.

I had no father around to tell me that I was beautiful. As a matter of fact, I had a poor self-image. I was dark skinned with huge eyes. My mom thought I had "good" hair and would not straighten it and my clothes were mostly hand made. I did not think I was pretty.

Upon entering high school, I became even more aware of material things (what I did not have). I visited my friends, who all seemed to live in better houses than me. It bothered me so much that I made a joke out of where I lived. It was a known fact that when you came to visit me, you had to call first because the family on the first floor had a mean little dog, who would scare you with his bark and actually bite you if given the chance. It was known that the set of stairs, which led to our floor was weak and you literally had to hold firm to keep from falling. One of my friends had a four-year-old niece who would say, "Carolyn, are you going home to your old raggedy house now?" Everyone would laugh and I would reply, "Yes, I am going home to my raggedy house now." No one knew how deeply that hurt. But, I saw it as a motivator for me to do better.

Although I may speak negatively about the way this house looked, it was indeed a home. It was a place of love, joy, and laughter. My brother and I were close and we spent a lot of time playing games and watching TV. We were inseparable. We would go to church together, spend weekends with our cousins together, and partner to sell paper Mother's Day roses each year. We would cover for each other when Mom went on the rampage and would whisper about her later, when we thought she couldn't hear us. My brother was the king of Kool-Aid.

When I was in eighth grade, the afro and the mini skirt were in style. I was able to get a beautiful curly afro that made me look very attractive and my body was nicely sculptured, with a tiny waist and big, pretty, shapely legs. I began to look pretty and feel pretty.

When I returned to school for my ninth grade year, I tried out for the cheerleading squad and I made it. I was always a nice person, but somewhat introverted. However, once I became a cheerleader, I was more outgoing and popular. My first real boyfriend and I lasted for about a year. When the relationship seemed to become too serious, I ended it. This became a trademark for me in high school, as I was determined that I would not get pregnant. I did not want to become a statistic. I wanted to escape from the circle of poverty that had been the history of my family. Even at that age, I knew my priorities. I saw pregnancy as a deterrent to attaining my goals.

Even though I mentioned my first boyfriend, I didn't know if I could take company because my mom and I had never had that discussion. As a matter of fact, we never had any conversations about the facts of life. However, do you remember Alice? She's the woman who cared for me as a child. She and I had those talks and she made sure I knew about the birds and the bees.

Although my mom worked the night shift, our onsite landlord was always on the job, watching everything that took place and knowing about any and everybody who came around. You see back in those days everyone looked out for everyone. If mom was not there, rest assured there was another adult somewhere looking out. That was a good thing! Maybe we could use more looking out and looking after in these days and times.

It was nothing to see many of my friends and schoolmates participating in promiscuous activities. Many were engaging in sex, having babies, and fighting in gangs. Pregnancy was prevalent, gangs existed, and life was challenging. When you grow up in a poor environment, it can be challenging to think big. But, I did. I knew that I wanted a better life. I knew that I wanted to contribute to society in a mighty way that pleased God.

As I started to wear platform shoes and high heels, I found myself wondering, "What would it mean to think big?" I knew I wanted better than what I had, but I didn't really know what was out there for me. I had always heard that education was the key to getting out of the ghetto. Therefore, it was important to me to do well in school, so that I could somehow go to college. We had no money so I would have to get a scholarship and/or student loan.

I was very active in high school: honor society, choir, social club, first runner up to Miss Charles A. Brown, and cheerleader. Thinking big to me, at that time, was graduating with honors. It was going to college and getting a good job. Marriage was not a part of my thought process. By the time I was in high school I had developed a negative impression of men. Based on my mom's experiences, I thought all men served as sperm donors to make babies and then disappear.

The man that I thought was my father came back into our lives when I was in high school. I was so happy to have a father that seemed to love me and I loved him. He called me scrappy. That was because as a little girl, my hair was so short that my mom had to literally scrap it together to make braids. My dad only stayed with us a short time (less than a year). I can vividly remember the night he left. He and my mom had an argument. I do not know what it was about, but I do think he had been out gambling and drinking. After their argument I heard him say, "I am out of here." Those words sparked a real pain in me. I ran into the room and grabbed my dad's leg and begged him to stay but he left anyway. That moment left an indelible mark on my life for a long time. From that point, I made up my mind that I would never let anyone get so close to hurt me again. In some way that incident was another thing that became negative motivation for me. At that young age I made a commitment to myself that I would not become a victim or another statistic. I was going to be the exception and not the norm.

High school graduation came and I did graduate with honors. Again, I began to wonder, "What does it mean to think big?" I met my goal of graduating high school. Now, I had to revise and expand my plan. I had to think bigger. My next goal was to go to college and graduate with honors. I began to wonder, "What college will I attend? What will I major in? What kind of career do I want?"

Well, I applied to two colleges and got accepted to both. I was selected to participate in a pre-freshman summer program at Saint Augustine's College (St. Aug) in Raleigh, NC and I totally loved it. I excelled in the classroom and enjoyed the social side of college life. My classmates and I really bonded and decided we were all going to return in the fall.

Upon my return, I decided to major in Business Management. Freshman year was successful. I adjusted well and made the Dean's List. During the summer I went home and was able to get a job at the U.S. Customs House.

I returned for my sophomore year. During this time, I continued to perform well academically. Gil and I became a couple. I joined Army ROTC and Gil was my platoon leader. While in ROTC, I was able to discover another side of me that was tough and military minded. This was the beginning of my wearing combat boots. I started my pledge process for Delta Sigma Theta Sorority, Incorporated. However, due to some problems, our line did not go over until the following year. I was also selected as Miss Alpha Phi Alpha Fraternity, Incorporated (Gamma Psi Chapter) and represented them on the queen's court at homecoming. I returned home for the summer and got my same job at the U. S. Custom's House.

My junior year was quite eventful. My line sisters and I crossed the burning sands of Delta Sigma Theta and I was elected Miss Saint Augustine's College. My reign would begin during the next school year. During that summer, I attended ROTC Advanced Camp and performed exceptionally well.

Finally, my senior year came and it was full of fun and excitement. Because of my performance and academic record, I was designated as the second in charge of our cadet battalion. I began my reign as campus queen, representing my school at official functions and serving as a role model of young womanhood. I found myself toggling between high heels and combat boots. But, I found that I wore both well. I was happy to meet another goal of graduating with honors and also receiving a commission as a second lieutenant in the United States Army.

Gil had graduated the year before me and was stationed at Fort Leonard Wood, Missouri. Upon graduation, I received an assignment to Fort Leonard Wood also. We had been dating for almost three years, some of which was long distance. There is an old adage that says, "absence makes the heart grow fonder." However, we decided that if I was unable to be assigned with him we would discontinue the relationship. Fortunately, the Army resolved this potential conflict by assigning me to my first choice. At that time I do not think many people requested Fort Leonard Wood, as it was in the middle of nowhere. As a matter of fact, the nick name for the post was "Fort Lost in the Woods, Misery." Well, this is the place where Gil and I got married. Shortly thereafter, we both received orders to go to Korea. However, he was assigned to one part of the country and I another. Gil and I visited each other on weekends. I can remember traveling on the chicken trains and the crowded buses to see my man.

Fort McPherson, GA, was our next assignment. This is where Summer was born. It was a cold Super Bowl Sunday. I believe we went to the doctor three times. The first time, the doctor sent us home indicating I had not dilated enough. The second time, I still was not ready, but the doctor suggested we go for a walk through the mall. The third time was the charm. The contractions were not yet within the ready zone but my water burst! This was reason enough to be admitted. I was in labor for fifteen hours. Gil and I had discussed natural birth. However, when those pains hit me, I yelled for an epidural. I am told that Gil instructed the doctor to not give me any drugs, as he and I had agreed on a natural birth. I am also told that I raised up from the bed, practically turned my neck 180 degrees like the demon-possessed girl in "The Exorcist," and with popped eyes and a seriously angry face made it clear that I was the one having this baby and that the doctor was going to go by my directions—not Gil's. I HAD AN EPIDURAL! And, we had a beautiful baby girl, 7 pounds 9 ounces. We had several other military assignments that took us from Indiana to Texas to Germany to North Carolina, where we retired. During these years, I had the pleasure of going from worn out shoes, to platforms, to combat boots, to high heels. They all fitted at the appropriate times, allowing me to show the flexibility and diversity that had become a part of me.

I dream of being a philanthropist one day, actively promoting human welfare. I decided to get started, even if it was in small doses. I have been contributing to charities for many years and decided that charity should also be done at home, when needed. As my mother has become old and very dependent on me, I have decided to make her a priority in my life. This has proven to be quite challenging, but it seems she has always anticipated the day that I would have to care for her. She tells the story of how she had five boys and she kept praying for a girl. Well, that girl is me.

My hope is to support seniors with my time, talent, and treasure. Having to care for my senior mother has made me even more sensitive to the plight of the aged in our society. My mom frequently says, "Once a woman, twice a child."

As I think big, I will one day have the opportunity to serve the senior population in a mighty way. But, until then, I will focus on providing the best care that I can to my elderly mother and spend quality time with her for as long as God allows.

As I continue to think big, I will pray that God continues to show me favor, so that I remain in His will and continue to experience His blessings, His grace, and His mercies. As I continue to think big, I will pray that my family is strong enough and selfless enough to reach out to others and share ourselves; to be care giver, friend, mentor, prayer partner, and disciple of Christ, as we grow in our walk with God.

As I continue to think big, I will pray that God allows me to journey to new places and old places that promote refueling, reenergizing, and restoring of my "soul." My journey will also involve meeting, greeting, and fellowshipping with people, who are part of my inner circle as well as with those who are not.

As I continue to think big, I will stride in my high heels, as I enjoy life—one day at a time. I want to honor God, as I continue to travel this road of life. I will wear many different kinds of shoes and pray that God's word is a lamp unto my feet and a light unto my path. As I think about my "*Soul to Sole: The Views from the Shoes,*" I want to live a life that is healthy in mind, body, and soul. I want to give my time, talent, and treasure to God and to those who are in need. I want to have knowledge and wisdom. As Proverbs 3:15-16 (KJV) says, "Wisdom is more precious than rubies. Nothing you desire can compare with her. She offers you long life in her right hand and riches and honor in her left. She will guide you down delightful paths; all her ways are satisfying."

As I think big, I imagine being a great author, who writes books that are relevant and inspiring. I imagine using the profits from these books to help others, especially seniors. I envision our business, "KNOWLES WHAT TO DO, LLC" becoming a great success. Currently, it is a small company, which provides substantive mentoring solutions that connect all generations. As a philanthropist, I envision expanding our focus on solutions for seniors—from senior day care to meals on wheels; from senior mentoring and reverse mentoring to senior spiritual and social outreach. I envision advocating for seniors in such a way that protects them from abuse, neglect, and exploitation. After having the opportunity and challenge to care for my aging mother, I have developed a passion and desire to support the needs of our senior population.

The bible says, "Honor thy father and thy mother and thy days will be long upon the land." I believe all of our elders are our mothers and fathers. Therefore, I believe we should serve and honor them as best we can.

CHAPTER 6

Shoes of a Woman

Most people say our daughter is a "daddy's girl." To me, she is also "mama's baby." Although Summer is now a woman she still seeks guidance, confirmation, and tenderness from me. I find it amazing that she and I tend to have some of the same experiences as we journey through the highs and lows of life. As I reflect upon the road I've traveled, there have been twists and turns where I have been bent but unbroken. I have been down but not out; distraught but not destroyed. As humans, we have a tendency to allow the bad to outshine the good. However, when I focus on the things for which I am thankful, I find that my mood changes. My stress level lowers or even disappears. I recommend this to any and all who will try it: think on things that are lovely.

As a mom, I counsel Summer to have great vision and dream big dreams. But reality will stare you in the face and you must prepare to thrive day by day. Notice I did not say survive. I said thrive! On the other hand, having a degree of control over what happens or fails to happen to me is critical in almost all situations I encounter. Don't get me wrong, I do know that God controls everything. However, I believe He expects me to do my part. To me, mom must be a model—an example of love, courage, strength, and wisdom.

I hear folks (especially men) say that Mother's Day is one of the most celebrated days of the year. I truly believe that if you have a mother who shows you love, you should love her back. If she has the courage to praise you when you are right and chide you when you are wrong, you should appreciate her. If you have a mother who has the strength to hold on and hold out, when giving up seems prudent, you should admire and cherish her. And, if you have a mother who is wise, you should definitely listen to her and respect her. You see, having a mom as a role model is biblical. Mom is that virtuous woman described in Psalm 31. She is not jealous of the love between a father and a daughter. Since I did not have a father in the home, I sometimes did not understand that special bond. However, I do know that it is a good thing. Summer has not had to seek the love of a man to fulfill a lack of love from her father. She knows she's beautiful; she knows she's smart; and, she knows she can do all things through Christ who strengthens her. Dad is an important part of a daughter's life, as he brings love from another perspective. Dad provides leadership and security, as well as stability and safety. But mom leverages all these things to make a house into a home.

In the midst of all this, things begin to shift. This realignment occurs when the daughter evolves into the model of womanhood. It may happen gradually or it may happen abruptly, but the result is the same. I now notice the true meaning of the old saying "out of the mouths of babes." The time has come to stop, look, and listen. We must heed the young, for it seems they have a raw truth that penetrates deeply.

How many of us allow our bodies to rule us? As women we have to go through quite a lot. When Eve gave that apple to Adam, could she even have imagined what she had done? As girl children, many of us begin our menstrual cycles by the age of twelve. For some, it starts even earlier than that. This is a sign of development into womanhood. Our bodies grow out and up. We sometimes become emotional and/or sensitive during our cycles. People may excuse our actions because "it's that time of the month." Well, for many women, menstrual cycles last into the 40's or 50's. Of course, there are exceptions. I discovered what perimenopause meant as I began going through changes in my sleep habits at the age of forty two.

Throughout my late forties my sleep habits increasingly worsened. The sleeplessness became more challenging and escalated to a level that was unsafe. It began to affect my focus, my mood, my attitude, and my overall well-being. My doctor prescribed medication to help me sleep.

It is amazing how perimenopause and full-blown menopause can affect so many aspects of your life. There are many symptoms associated with both. Here are all of the ones that I have experienced: hot flashes, night sweats, irritability and mood swings; sleeplessness, fatigue, anxiety, difficulty focusing and memory lapses; aching and sore joints, muscles and tendons; breast tenderness, indigestion, nausea, bouts of bloat, weight gain and hair thinning; changes in body odor, tingling in the extremities, ringing in the ears and softer fingernails that easily crack and break. You might ask, what did you not experience? And I would not blame you. I am still on this journey. It's not as bad as it has been, but several of the aforementioned symptoms still occur.

Seeking relief, I have purchased several personal fans and have placed one in each of my pocketbooks, book bags, and brief cases. You see, I would break out into an embarrassing sweat at any time. I placed electric fans throughout the house. In the bedroom there are two electric fans going most of the time. I would lower the temperature in the house to a comfortable level for me, but this would make Gil feel cold. In my office at work I have the air conditioner on all year round. My colleagues often remarked that it felt like the North Pole.

As time has passed, I still struggle with bouts of night sweats, but the hot flashes have significantly subsided and the other symptoms have become infrequent. I am so glad that I did not take the prescribed hormone medication. It has been a long, hard road, but I do believe the worst of it is behind me. I look forward to this new chapter in my life and pray that God will lead, guide and continue to bring me through in a mighty way.

CHAPTER 7

He Restores My Soul

Sometimes you just need a place to go for a weekend "get-away." Sometimes you need to have your soul restored and your soles repaired. This reminds me of one of my favorite bible passages that I learned as a child. Psalm 23 is the framework of this entire book. It could be summarized as: He Restores My Soul.

PSALM 23
A Psalm of David
The Holy Bible
(KJV)

The LORD is my shepherd; I shall not want.
He maketh me to lie down in green pastures:
he leadeth me beside the still waters.
He restoreth my soul: he leadeth me in the
paths of righteousness for his name's sake.
Yea, though I walk through the valley of the
shadow of death,
I will fear no evil: for thou art with me; thy
rod and thy staff they comfort me.

Thou preparest a table before me in the
presence of mine enemies: thou anointest
my head with oil; my cup runneth over.
Surely goodness and mercy shall follow me all
the days of my life: and I will dwell in the house
of the LORD for ever.

To restore means to return to the original and/or useable and
functioning condition. I had a pair of beautiful black shoes, which
were favorites of mine. Not only were they beautiful but they were
also comfortable, especially for high heels. One day while wearing
them, I felt the sole on the right foot flap. I took the shoe off to
realize the sole was peeling away from the shoe. I then looked at the
left foot and saw the same thing was beginning to happen. I became
saddened to think I may have to throw away these shoes. Then Gil
said it may be worth taking the shoes to a local shoe repair shop.
After searching the Internet for "shoe repair" in our zip code, one
popped up that was less than ten miles away from our home. Gil
took these shoes to the shoe repair and the very next day he was able
to pick them up. To my delight, the shoes looked brand new. My
soles were restored.

Sometimes we feel like we are peeling away from the base that keeps
us connected. Some of us suffer in silence, as we struggle to keep
it all together. As I stop and reflect, I can remember being blessed
with many periods of restoration. Every day that God allows me
to awaken and witness the beauty of His holiness, I am restored.
To get peaceful and restful sleep brings about restoration for the
mind, body and soul. When I walk through the valley, there is joy
in knowing that I am going "through" valleys in order to get "to"
mountains. My shoes may get worn and even torn as I tarry from
here to there. But, His rod is there to comfort me.

CHAPTER 8

Guide My Footsteps

In one of the many powerful sermons preached by my pastor, Reverend Doctor Howard-John Wesley of Alfred Street Baptist Church in Alexandria, VA, he said "If you are not going to move, then don't ask God to guide your footsteps." I found that to be quite profound. Of all the parts of our bodies, the parts that move us most effectively and efficiently are our feet. Although our hands and knees can help our bodies move, they are not most effective. Footsteps are God's intended ways for humans to move. Our feet can take us to many places. Some are holy places and some are not. My mother-in-law loved the hymn entitled, "Higher Ground," where it says, "Lord plant my feet on higher ground." To me, being planted on higher ground means being secured with a place in heaven. It means planting seeds on earth of the fruit of the spirit, which are love, joy, peace, kindness, goodness, gentleness, faithfulness, patience, and discipline.

As I move in and around God's earth, I must love everyone and follow the Golden Rule to do unto others as I would have them do unto me. I must not only be happy, but I must spread joy to those with whom I have contact. There is a big difference between happiness and joy. People and things can make you happy or unhappy. But, only God can give you joy, which comes from the inside and flows to the outside. A writer once said, "What's inside of you will come out of you and will affect everyone around you." That God-given joy can help you to see the cup half full instead of half empty. Joy can help you smile when you really want to cry. And, when you do cry, you can shed tears of joy.

Where are some of the places my feet have gone? What did my feet do when they got there? What happens when you have no feet? Well, my feet have taken me to many places. Some include places of schooling and professional development; places like kindergarten, elementary, and high school; colleges and universities; military institutions; and other training sites. My feet have taken me to places for spiritual uplifting and wellbeing; places like Sunday School and church; Christian Youth Fellowship, prayer meetings, bible study, and Vacation Bible School. My feet have also taken me to social places; places like clubs and dance halls; parties, football and basketball games, as well as track meets. My feet have walked, run, danced, shouted, kicked, and jumped. Today, they continue to stand.

Have you ever been in a situation where you said, "Feet don't fail me now." It could have been when you were afraid and you were running away from something or someone; it could have been when you were playing or participating in a running sport, such as track, football, basketball, or even activities like ice skating, roller skating, hockey, or tennis. We all have done some things that required our feet to be the dominant body part. It's amazing how we take things for granted. Some of us may remember squeezing our size nine feet into size eight shoes. That may have appeared cute when we were younger. But, when the bunions and corns appeared, we had proof that we made a bad decision earlier in life. Now, when we want to wear the cute shoes that expose our toes, we may give it a second thought. Thank God for nail polish and pedicures!

Feet are made to take footsteps. But, what if you had no feet? Some people are born with deformities or conditions that may impact their feet and how well they are able to move. You may have heard of people having pigeon toes, slew feet, bowlegs, and club feet. These conditions affect the way you look and move. I can remember when I was growing up, I wanted to be bowlegged. I thought that was the cutest thing because I have knock knees. I hated being knock-kneed. In the 1970's the mini's were in style (mini-skirts, mini-dresses, and mini-shorts). I had big, pretty legs and I looked good in a mini. But I had knock knees and thought that took away from my overall look. However, as time passed, the style changed from mini's to maxi's. I was only 5'3" and I thought taller people looked better in these long skirts and dresses. It seems humans are just so hard to please.

Whether you wore a mini or maxi, the shoes you wore helped to make the outfit. The shoes could dress it up or dress it down. Once you were ready to step out, the prayer was always that God would guide your footsteps and help you to go places that did not lead you into danger or distress.

There is a saying, "walk a mile in my shoes," which means you need to understand my perspective. Basically, the shoes I wear belong to me. They are a perfect fit on my feet and they are responsible for covering my soles as I journey here and there. They may be too tight, and cause blisters, which impact the quality of my journey. They may also be too big, which also can cause problems that impact the quality of my walk. No one can really know how I feel while I'm wearing my shoes.

Some people may have traveled the same road, but still my journey is personal. People may give me advice; warn me with a yellow or red flag; and even suggest surrender. However, it's up to me to heed the warnings or suffer the consequences. There are times when I have to take a stand or choose to walk away. There are some fights worth fighting and there are others that are not. Sometimes you run, but you cannot hide. That's when you really need to know that God sits high and looks low. He sees all things and has the power to lead us and guide us, if we ask. He is always willing to aid us and forgive us when we take bad turns on the road of life. But, we have to have a relationship with Him. We have to be able to talk to Him . . . to pray to Him. He is a loving father who knows His children and always has open arms. The bottom line is, if you're not going to move, then don't ask God to guide your footsteps.

Part III

Summer's Time

Summer's Time

By
Carolyn Knowles

Born in the winter, but Summer is her name;
on a cold day in January, this bundle of joy came.
Dad immediately checked for all of her fingers and toes,
upon realizing God's blessing, joy overflowed.

Summer's Time is like January's carnation;
it is a time of love, distinction, and fascination.
Carnations come in several beautiful colors,
pink, red, white, green, purple, and yellow.

Summer's Time is about overcoming hurdles that life brings;
it is about learning, growing, and moving
on to bigger and better things.
Summer's Time is about belonging to the Y Generation;
it is about grooming the new leaders of our great nation.

During Summer's Time, the living will be easy;
during Summer's Time, the struggle will be done.
During Summer's Time, all the generations
will stand together; and
during Summer's Time, the victory will be won.

CHAPTER 9

The Early Years

My name is Summer Knowles. I was born on January 24, 1982 . . . on Super Bowl Sunday. My arrival demanded my father's attention away from the game and everything else for that matter. In hindsight, the day of my birth foreshadowed my life in two ways. First, how blessed with athletic ability I would be and how it would shape my early years. Second, whether good or bad, it was a preview of my affinity for the spotlight.

When I started to think about the shoes that best represented my early school and college years, the answer immediately came to mind—my track spikes! For those of you unfamiliar with what those are, they are running shoes. However, they aren't just any running shoes. They are normally only used for competition, or maybe a high-level practice before competition. They are exactly how they sound, lightweight running shoes with spikes screwed into the bottom, which improve your traction on a rubber track.

There was a time in my life when track was king, or queen, I should say. High school is often a very difficult time for teens, as they shape their self-image, and I was no exception. The lessons I learned about people and life in general during my high school track years, aka my spike years, really shaped my life.

I was new to a small private school for rich kids, who had attended school together since pre-kindergarten and the only Black female in my class, which ended up being the case all four years. Yes, my high school experience was challenging.

I was what we call a military brat. Both of my parents were in the army and so we moved around often. The army bases we lived on were great, and very diverse. My best friends growing up were Black, White, Iranian and Hispanic. Honestly, it wasn't until my parents retired to Raleigh, NC, where I attended middle and high school that I realized race was kind of a big deal, or at least in the south.

I had friends at school and I got along well with other students there but those friendships only existed during school hours or during school activities. Although I lived in an upper middle class neighborhood most of those kids didn't have much contact with African Americans. I became the designated representative for all Black females, and a lot of times for the entire Black race. I was annoyed and offended by the constant questions about why they had to attend a Black history month program for 30 minutes once a year. They would say things like, "It's not fair; it's really reverse discrimination because there is no white history month." I remember one student telling me that, standing there in his Confederate tee shirt and matching belt buckle.

There was at least one teacher who seemingly shared her beliefs, and let's just say her class was a major pain. In hindsight, I should have called her to task on some of the things she pulled in class. But, I digress.

I often felt alone. There was one Black guy in my class, who I remember having a crush on and dating very shortly, but he was more into White girls. Therefore, for the most part, it was a cold, isolating situation. But, my saving grace at the school, or at least I thought at the time . . . was my track coach, who was also my English teacher. He was, and I believe still is the only African American teacher at the school. I never really talked to him about the isolation I felt, but somehow, whether it was true or something I just made up in my head, I felt he understood my plight.

I have always been a good runner. I can remember, during my elementary school years, when I raced my classmates, I usually won the sprints and enjoyed the spirit of competition, especially the thrill of victory.

While in high school, track was one of my first, and really my only, strong interests. Steven McGill, my new track coach, seemed thrilled to have me join his team. Everything was great. I won multiple state championships my freshman year and had an equally successful sophomore year, even picking up a new event . . . the 100-meter hurdles. The hurdles started out only as a way for me to get more of his time, but ended up being my first love. However, that ended as most first loves do—in heartbreak.

Track was my only social outlet at school and my only real bonding time with my coach. As I mentioned earlier, he was also my English teacher and the only real friend I felt I had at the school. But, that came to an end the summer after my sophomore year, when I tore my anterior cruciate ligament (ACL) in my right knee. I would never run the same again.

Ultimately, in the weeks leading up to my surgery, and the week or two that I was out of school after my surgery, my relationship with McGill deteriorated. He never called. He never inquired as to how I

75

was doing—not just physically, but emotionally. I was a mess as far as both were concerned. And when I finally got back on the track after nearly a year of rehab, it wasn't the same. I was not the same. And McGill never treated me the same. His actions, or the lack thereof, were of betrayal, and something I would never forgive. At least that is what I thought at that time.

I did eventually forgive him for the letdown, but it took years. Honestly, even to this day, which is more than a decade later, when I think about it I still feel something. It was a year or so after graduating college (UNC-Chapel Hill), where I had a full, four-year track scholarship that I ran across something McGill had written about the situation in his online track blog.

It explains how everything went down from his perspective and ultimately helped me heal . . . us heal . . . after the thing that really solidified our friendship tore us apart. The piece was entitled, "Days of Summer." McGill gave me permission to use it in this book and it follows in the next chapter.

CHAPTER 10

Days of Summer

By
Steven McGill

Sometimes, the most important stories to tell are the hardest ones to tell. Such is the case for me when it comes to the best female hurdler I've ever coached. We had a lot of success together, but our relationship fell apart during her senior year, and we have only recently begun to piece it back together. There is no short way to tell this story, so let me go back to the beginning:

In 1997, the first truly gifted athlete that I had the opportunity to coach—Summer Knowles—entered my life. She was a freshman sprinter who had transferred from a nearby public school. With very quick turnover for a relatively tall girl (5'8"), Summer was an instant success in the sprints, finishing first in the 100 and second in the 200 at the North Carolina Independent Schools State Championships. She went on to run for the Durham Striders—a track club based in Durham, NC—throughout the summer, further improving upon the success she had achieved during the school season.

In the fall of the following year, her sophomore year, she asked me to teach her how to hurdle. I was hesitant at first, because we already had good depth in the hurdles, and we needed her to continue leading us in the sprints. But she was persistent, so I agreed to teach her, and Summer picked up on it very quickly. She was an eager learner, and a very hard worker. In the winter months, we'd often be out on the track until it was too dark to see, doing drills, smoothing out technical problems. I remember that she fell twice in practice during the off-season, and that, both times, she got back up and continued on. One thing I noticed, with some frustration, was that the more I tried to instruct her in a hands-on manner, the more confused she became. There was one practice when I didn't even run myself at all, although, back then, I would always run with my athletes. On this day, however, I devoted all my time to watching Summer and trying to help her improve. Nothing worked—until the end of practice, when I left her alone and was talking to another athlete who had finished his workout. Summer, on her own, started doing one of the drills I had shown her earlier, then after doing that a couple times, went back to sprinting over the hurdles. This time she cleared them all, and was able to instantly apply the drill to the actual hurdling. That practice ended on a positive note. So, in a workout a couple days later, I told her I would leave her alone and let her teach herself how to hurdle, since she seemed to be doing a better job at it than I was. She had another great practice, and was really beginning to look comfortable and natural going over hurdles.

Around that time, it was becoming obvious to me that a beautiful story was developing. Summer said something to me late in the practice that I'll never forget. I was explaining something technical to her and asked her if she understood. "Yeah, I understand," she said, "but now I just have to *do* it." It was then when I realized I needed to back off and give her the space she needed to figure this hurdling thing out for herself. Before then, I'd been pressing too much; I'd been too worried that maybe hurdling was something

Summer wouldn't be able to pick up. That's why I was being so hands-on—I wanted to ensure that this project would work. But when I let go is when things started to actually fall in place for her; that's when she began to learn how to hurdle. She taught herself something by *doing* it; she learned it through repetition. Those winter months taught me a valuable lesson: sometimes I do my best coaching when I'm not really coaching at all, when I'm letting the athletes coach themselves; sometimes I do my best coaching when I trust them, and give them room to explore.

In the first outdoor meet—a small meet at Durham Academy, one of our rivals—Summer ran a very sloppy race, zigzagging all over the lane, hitting a lot of hurdles. She gave me a distraught look afterwards, as if asking me what had gone wrong. I didn't have any answers, so I just kind of stared emptily back at her. We were both surprised when the official hand-timing her said she had run a 14.9. I assumed it had to be a mistake. But it wasn't.

As the season wore on, Summer's technique got better and better, and she grew more aggressive and more confident. Meanwhile, her times in the open 100 and 200 were also coming down as well, although I didn't really have her doing all that much speed work. It seemed that the improvements in her hurdling form were creating improvement in her running form without us needing to focus on it. In the state meet that year, she won three events—the 100, the 200, and the 100 hurdles, all in record times. Her time in the hurdles was 14.40, which ranked her among the top two in the state, and among the top fifty in the nation at that point in the year. It was very rewarding for me to see her do so well. It verified to me that all those cold days in the winter months had been worthwhile, and that an athlete with exceptional natural talent and a work ethic to match has limitless potential.

During the summer, Summer ran with the Durham Striders again. I was thinking about joining their coaching staff so that I could continue coaching Summer as I had all year, and I even went to one of their practices. But they already had a hurdle coach, so I felt like I just didn't fit into the picture. Unlike both of us had thought, her times didn't come down during the summer months. She got stuck in the 14.5 range, and didn't improve her personal record until the final meet of the season, running a 14.32 at nationals. I felt like I had let her down, and I felt like some distance had been created between us. I had been there for her throughout the winter and the spring, but when she really needed me, when she was facing the heavy competition of the summertime meets, I was nowhere to be found. All spring long we had talked about how her times would come down once she had tough competition to run against regularly. But it didn't really happen. At that time, I simply didn't yet realize how good of a coach I was. The fact that Summer learned how to hurdle primarily by teaching herself is something I viewed as proof that I really had little to do with her success. I didn't realize then what I came to realize much later—that silently observing her and allowing her to teach herself was actually a very effective method of coaching. I assumed that I pretty much just got lucky that things turned out so well. I assumed that her times would come down even further once the summer season started and she had stiffer competition and more experienced coaches.

One of the biggest mistakes I made in regard to my relationship with Summer, and it started during that summer between her sophomore and junior years, was in not taking a more hands-on approach, in not saying that she was my athlete. I didn't want to be an ego-tripper going around shouting "Look at this girl that *I* coach," but it just goes to show that being humble can sometimes have its drawbacks; sometimes humility is just a veiled way of not accepting the responsibility that comes with being relied upon. That was a major mistake I made in regard to my relationship with Summer.

In a journal that I kept around that time, I wrote the following thoughts:

Maybe I should have stayed helping with the Striders even if I wouldn't have had that much authority; at least I could have been there as someone to talk to, someone to keep her confidence up. Maybe I should have told her the hell with the Striders, you're training with me. Too busy being nice and diplomatic. My flaw right now is that I'm afraid to be really good at what I do. Why am I surprised that Summer's times didn't keep getting better after she stopped training with me? Don't I realize how good a coach I am? Why did I think she could pick up where she left off without my being there? Why do I assume that because other coaches were better athletes than me in their day, they're automatically gonna be better coaches than me as well? Why do I assume that simply because other coaches have been involved in coaching longer than I have, that they can bring out the best in their athletes better than I can? Why can't I see that coaching the hurdles is my gift, that it's what I'm good at? What am I afraid of?

The thing about it is, everything Summer and I did during those winter and spring months worked. I was too involved in it at the time to realize it—too involved in monitoring the emotional damage done to all my other female hurdlers by the mere fact that Summer was hurdling at all, too involved in the hopes and the maybes and the what-ifs of Summer's slow progress, too involved in stressing myself out over unmotivated runners on the team who, in retrospect, really weren't worth worrying about. But I could see it now. Everything we did worked. So, I resolved, as Summer headed into her junior year, that I, and only I, would be her coach. Together, as soon as school started up again in late August, we made up a list of goals. I also devised and gave her a workout plan to follow throughout the year. Both of us were eager about the prospect of her breaking 14.00 in the 100 hurdles, and of breaking 12.00 in the open 100.

Then, one day in September, I heard the news . . . Summer hurt her knee fooling around playing touch football after school. At first the doctors thought it was her meniscus, and she would have to get it operated on, but there was a chance she might be ready for the spring season. Still, it seemed apparent that any goals we had had in mind for her would have to be put on hold. A week later, she had an MRI done, and the news was worse. She tore her anterior cruciate ligament. She would miss the whole season.

Summer missed about a week of school after her surgery, during which time I did not communicate with her at all. It was the end of the first grading quarter, so I was busy computing grades and writing grade reports in addition to the regular everyday teacher stuff I always had to do. I didn't have time to call Summer. A couple days after her return she came to talk to me, and said that she felt I had abandoned her. As a mentor, she said, I had abandoned her. She was on the verge of crying. I was upset as well. She mentioned how I had kept in touch with her over the summer and how she had called me from Maryland after the East Coast Invitational, and now that she really needed me, it seemed like I just didn't care. What could I say? She had the right to feel that I had abandoned her. Looking back, I wonder myself why I didn't even call to see how the operation went. Was I that busy with school stuff that I couldn't pick up the phone? I always pride myself on my ability to focus on the things that really matter, and to not allow myself to get caught up in the trivial things that only seem very important. This was one instance in which I had allowed the thing that really mattered to go overlooked.

I taught Summer American Literature that entire year, so I saw her every day. As the school year progressed, she seemed to struggle more and more with the fact that she couldn't run. She suffered a lot that year, having to read newspaper articles about other local track athletes throughout the season, and having to hear about how good other girls were doing for our team. Summer came to a couple of our meets early in the year, but stopped coming after the second or third one. I didn't make her come; I wanted her to feel like a part of the team, but I knew it was hard for her to watch so many races that she would've been winning had she been healthy.

Losing a whole year to injury broke her heart. In the conversations I had with her, she expressed anxiety over the possibility that she would lose all scholarship opportunities that she otherwise would have had, and she also expressed sorrow over the fact that she had lost a huge chunk of her identity. "I used to be a track star," she said to me quite matter-of-factly on one of her darker days, "now I'm nobody." On days when her frustration reached its peak, she was especially caustic. I remember one day, while we were discussing The Great Gatsby in class, Summer kept saying, "This book is dumb." Well, it's not my favorite book either, so I wasn't going to argue its value just because I was the teacher, but she kept on saying, "This book is dumb. Why are we reading it? What are we reading next? I hate this book." It's like she was trying to get a reaction from me. I remember one time she complained because I took off points on a test for spelling a character's name wrong. "I can't believe you took off points for that," she snapped. "The name's in the book, Summer," I retorted, "why don't you be quiet and read the book." She stopped fussing after that. I knew that Summer was really upset about not being able to run—not about some stupid test—and that she was just taking her frustrations out on me because neither she nor I could do anything about it. But when Summer is in pain she puts up walls, and when she does it's virtually impossible to communicate with her. All one can do is wait till she takes the wall down.

Toward the end of her junior year, Summer began coming to practice and working out on her own, sprinting as fast as her knee would allow her to. She generally did 100 or 150 or 200 meter sprints, with lots of rest between reps. It was good to see her out there again, and it was hard not to think of what might have been. One day she was doing some 150s with another one of our girl sprinters who was also recovering from an injury. Summer, needing more recovery between reps, fell behind, and ended up having to do the last one by herself. She asked me to time it, and I did. By that point in the practice, the only people still on the track were Summer, myself, and Steve Cockburn (pronounced Co-burn), who had just finished an extensive 110 hurdle workout. So Cockburn and I were standing at the finish line as Summer ran her 150—he exhorting her to run faster, and me yelling out the time. I remember looking at her round the curve and surge into the straightaway and thinking to myself, "Good Lord, she's rolling." There was a look of determination on her face, a look that told me that, in her mind, she was running more than an ordinary practice sprint; she was reclaiming her territory, she was beginning her comeback. She ended up running that last repeat in something like 18 or 19 seconds—faster than anybody on our team had done that day, male or female. Afterward, exhausted, she lay on the track to catch her breath. Eventually, she sat up, but didn't stand up. "Next year began today," I said to Steve, "The year 2000 began today." Hearing me, Summer smiled through her fatigue, and Cockburn laughed, sharing my enthusiasm. The three of us talked a little while longer, and then I left, and then Cockburn left. I remember, after I had gone to the locker room and showered and changed, I was on my way out to my car when I peeped through the window and saw Summer still sitting there, where Cockburn and I had left her, alone, on the track. I was going to go back out there and talk to her some more, or at least ask her why she was still sitting there. But I decided not to; I knew why she was still there. She needed to be.

In Summer's senior year, things fell apart rapidly. She was told that her knee was all better, but that it would be dangerous for her to try to hurdle on it. That meant that the root cause of us forming such a close bond—the hurdles—could no longer be our primary source of connection. She would have to run only the sprints, and probably have to move up to the 400, as running the 100 would also put a great deal of strain on her knee. In the fall of her senior year, around the same time that she was told she couldn't hurdle, she accepted a scholarship offer to UNC-Chapel Hill. Her times from her sophomore year were fast enough to merit the scholarship. Although she had started doing some conditioning stuff beforehand, I didn't see much of her on the track after that. I wasn't teaching her anymore, so it was harder to find her during the day.

My assumption was, now that she couldn't hurdle anymore, she had lost a lot of her motivation. Summer worked hard when it came to learning how to hurdle, but, with her knee, she couldn't hurdle anymore unless she got it operated on again. I really don't think that Summer enjoyed running. She enjoyed competing, and she thrived on winning, but she didn't enjoy running itself. And without hurdles in her way, it seemed that her ability to motivate herself had gone away. Because, in her sophomore year, when she first started hurdling, no one on our team worked harder than Summer. I'm sure she was thinking that I felt she decided to slack off and rest on her laurels once she got her scholarship to UNC, although that's not how I felt at all. The problem was, regardless of how I felt, or why she stopped coming to practice, we didn't communicate with each other. We just allowed ourselves to drift apart. I don't know what her mindset may have been, but mine was that I shouldn't have to chase her or seek her out; if she wants to run, she knows where the track is; if she wants to talk, she knows where my office is. I put my pride before our relationship, as I'm sure she did as well, and we both suffered as a result.

One day in early February, as it was getting closer to the spring season, I called her at home just to see what was going on with her, and to find out if her mind was still focused on track. She said she had been running with her mom, that she knew I probably thought she hadn't been doing anything at all, but that she was going to show me once the season started. It surprised me that I had become an antagonistic figure in her mind. She was going to show *me*? I had thought that *we* were going to show the world. By the time the outdoor season began, it seemed obvious to me that Summer and I would never be as close as we once had been. She could be a difficult person to approach, and I must admit that I could be too, as much as I tried not to be. Also, the fact that she wasn't hurdling created a rift in our relationship that we just couldn't seem to overcome. She said to me early in the season that she didn't feel that I was her coach as much as she used to because she wasn't hurdling anymore. Although I voiced my disagreement, in my heart I knew she was right. On days that hurdlers worked on technique, I was with them. Those used to be the days when Summer and I would bond. They still remained the days when I would bond with my hurdlers. But Summer wasn't one of them now, so it was different.

Meanwhile, her times in the sprints were surprisingly fast in the early part of the year. She ran a hand-timed 25.4 in the 200 and 12.3 in the 100. Summer's attitude had definitely changed, though. I needed her to be to a leader, a captain, since she was a senior with a lot of experience. But because she had missed her entire junior year, she wanted to focus on herself, to make up for the time she had missed, so she didn't want to be bothered with the rest of the team. She was anxious to be done with high school and to get on to UNC. She started missing practices, explaining that training with the girls on our team wasn't making her any better. Plus, her habit of taking a whole lot of rest between interval reps wasn't stopping. We had a very immature team that year, so I needed someone to show some leadership, but Summer, by that time, was too self-absorbed, too bitter, and too plain old mad at the world to be that person. She ran a very good 4x400 leg at the Penn Relays in April, and we had a lot of fun on that trip. She and I had our first and only really good conversation of the season in the hotel lobby on the night before the race, and I was beginning to feel confident that, hurdles or no hurdles, we might be able to salvage something of substance out of this season after all.

But Summer's times in the sprints weren't getting any faster, and toward the latter part of the season, she began to despair. At the state meet, she was scheduled to run the 100, 200, and 400. Without consulting me, she took herself out of the 400 so that she could gear up and try to win the shorter sprints. It didn't work. She finished second in the 100, and she finished third in the 200. In both races, she lost to girls that the pre-ACL Summer would have blown away. In both races, her running form fell apart at the end. She was making a swimming motion with her arms, as if she were reaching for the finish line, but she just couldn't get there soon enough. After the 200, I tried to console her. I walked up to her and patted her on the back. When she turned around and saw who it was she said, "Get away from me, McGill, you haven't given a ____ about me all season." Those were the last words she spoke to me that day, and, at that moment, I felt that they may very well be the last words she would ever speak to me. Too hurt to respond, I walked silently away.

I remember thinking to myself, on the bus ride home to Raleigh after that meet, about the scar on her knee—the scar from the surgery, and how it symbolically represented our relationship. When she had been running the hurdles, our relationship had been whole, complete, and everything had been going well. Just like her knee. But after the surgery, just like she never returned to her old running form, and just like she never ran the hurdles again, the relationship between Summer and myself never fully recovered, never fully healed, but instead remained permanently scarred. Even though at times during the season it was good, it never got back to being as good as it once had been. Every time, during the latter part of the season, when I would glance down at her knee, I would think about that. And then, at the state meet, "Get away from me McGill . . . ." It all fell apart. It all fell apart.

Throughout her career at UNC, Summer was never fully healthy. Injuries plagued her the whole time she was there. Her sophomore year of high school ended up being her best year of running track. I kept up with her progress by looking up meet results on-line, by talking to another UNC track athlete I knew, and by hearing from other alums who still kept in touch with Summer. I didn't call her, I didn't email her, I didn't try to communicate with her in any manner. As far as I was concerned, our relationship was over. It had been fractured beyond repair, and even though I didn't like the fact, I accepted that I would have to live with it.

But I couldn't live with it. It took me three years to let go of enough of my anger and pride to admit to myself that I still cared about her. In the middle of the night one night, I wrote her an email—a long letter in which I tried to repair the broken bridges that lie in crumbled ruins between us. I didn't know for sure if she would even respond at all. I thought she might see who it was from and delete it without even reading it. But a few days later, she did respond. It was a bitter letter in which she basically let out three years' worth of pent-up anger. We were still oceans apart from each other. In her email, she expressed her disbelief that I couldn't understand why she felt that I had betrayed her. From my end, I resented the fact that I had made the attempt to reach out my hand to her, and she had responded by biting it. We were still very far apart.

I tried again, last year, her senior year at UNC. Her response was less bitter. It seemed that the ice was thawing, so to speak. I emailed her again in the summer, informally asking her how her season turned out, and what her plans were now that she had graduated college. I received a very nice email in return in which she expressed forgiveness, the desire for closure, and she even had some plain old, normal conversation in there about how much she liked her new job. In October of 2004, she came to our homecoming football game, and I saw her again for the first time in five years. We hugged, we got caught up on each other a bit, and we talked like two human beings who actually like each other. It was cool, to say the least. It was very cool.

Of all the lessons I have learned from all the emotional upheavals of my relationship with Summer, the one that stands out the most in my mind is that girls and boys cannot be coached the same way. It sounds like a rather basic thing to say, maybe even an ignorant thing to say, but it has become so obvious to me that I cannot deny the truth of it. With boys, performance comes first, and the relationship comes second. Help me to get better, is what boys want. Help me to get faster; help me to win races. If a male athlete sees no improvement in his performance, even though he's doing everything the coach tells him to do, that athlete will lose faith in his coach, and the relationship will deteriorate. But if the athlete's performance does steadily improve, and victories mount, that bond between coach and athlete will strengthen, even if they aren't "buddy-buddy." A male coach, similarly, wants to see a work ethic before he commits himself to investing time in an athlete. Work your butt off and I'll do anything for you. But if you don't show the willingness to put in the work required to compete at a certain level, the male coach will basically look elsewhere for someone who will. So, between a male coach and a male athlete, there is an unspoken understanding, from both perspectives: performance comes first.

Female athletes, on the other hand, want to know that they matter to you; they want to be sure that you care about them. Once they have that assurance, they will work as hard as asked. So, the problems I had with Summer were really only an extreme version of the problems that have arisen, at one point or another, with just about every girl I've ever coached. I've come to realize that not every man is fit to coach female athletes, and I must admit I've had my own doubts as to whether or not I'm equipped to do so. Maybe I am too competitive, maybe I am too focused on winning to have the patience to be nurturing and comforting when the situation calls for it. The Summer drama has really forced me to look at myself in the mirror.

Since the days of Summer, I handle differences with female athletes differently than I used to. I make it a point now to give my female athletes lots of attention, to give them a hug after every race, even if I'm disappointed with their performance, and to make sure I have informal conversations with them whenever I can, even if I don't feel they're practicing as hard as I feel they need to. With female athletes, I make a conscious effort to put the relationship first, and it has made a difference. In the past five years, I've had relationships with several female athletes that most certainly would have fallen apart if I didn't have the memory of Summer Knowles in my mind to guide me. The whole Summer fiasco has made me a better coach, and that's one positive I can take from it. I do also feel that if she and I can remain friends and stay in touch with each other in the coming years, then the pain of those long, dark years of misunderstanding will fade away.

© 2004 Steve McGill

CHAPTER 11

From Track Shoes to Stilettos

I am now at another phase of my life. I have been out of college for almost 10 years. I am in a challenging television broadcasting career. My first job was in Charlotte, NC, at Channel 4, where I initially worked in archiving, and then moved on the production side. It's amazing how opportunity works. I remember going to visit a friend, who worked as a reporter at a TV station in Charlottesville, VA. It just so happened, this was during the Christmas holidays and weather was bad. Several reporters were unable to make it back from their vacation. I had an opportunity to fill in as a reporter for a few days and did a good job. Well, a job became available at that station less than six months later—and guess what—I got the job. This was my first real job as a reporter. I learned quite a bit, as I had to do everything. It was what we call a "One Man Band" operation.

I worked at this station for two years. When my contract was up, I interviewed with several stations and landed an awesome opportunity at a station in St. Louis, MO. I moved from a market that was #187 to a market that was #21. In my field, that rarely happens. This was big! Of course I had some doubts about moving up so fast, but my family and I prayed about it (as we do about all things) and off to St. Louis I went. My Dad and I drove from Virginia to Missouri. You see, my Dad is awesome. He is always there for me. For this move and every move I have made, this has been bonding time for he and I. Mom usually comes shortly thereafter to help me get settled in.

The director who hired me for the reporter job in Missouri left for another job a few months after my arrival. This presented many challenges for me. I was under the impression that he would be there to mentor me, since he knew I was not yet very experienced. Well, I guess that's the way the cookie crumbles. Needless to say, when the new director came on board, she was not about mentoring. She expected me to know what to do and to do it well. I worked many long and hard hours during this time. Being the new person, it was nothing for me to work all weekends and holidays! I was far away from home—extremely lonely and homesick. I wanted to quit, but my parents continually encouraged, motivated, and inspired me to at least complete my contract, then decide whether I wanted to leave the field or not. As time passed, I met a couple of senior reporters/anchors, who advised and guided me when needed. With the grace of God, I made it through those three years.

From St. Louis, I was blessed to get a job with a TV station in West Palm Beach, FL, as a reporter. I was truly excited to be back in the south. As a matter of fact, my Dad is from Miami and it was a little over an hour drive from West Palm Beach. I do believe all things are designed by God. While in West Palm Beach, I had the opportunity to spend quality time with my grandma (Dad's Mom) as an adult. I would drive down and cook for her. We would sit around, watch TV, and talk. I am so happy for those days, as my grandma passed away while I was working in West Palm Beach.

Again, to show you how the Lord works, I was only in West Palm Beach for a little over a year, when an anchoring opportunity became available in Shreveport, LA. Because of this great opportunity, I was able to get out of my contract and move on to Shreveport. Again, my

Dad and I packed up and drove from Florida to Louisiana. Mom came later to help me settle in to my new place.

Being the morning anchor and also a reporter was a new and challenging experience. However, once again, I was away from family and friends, who nurtured and inspired me. Our ratings were usually good and I did learn much about the industry while I was there.

As I was approaching the end of my contract, my agent set up several interviews for me and I had several offers from which to choose. I was about to accept an offer in North Carolina, when Miami called. After weighing the pros and cons of each offer, I decided to accept the reporter job with CBS in Miami (#16 market). After all, it was a big international market, with much promise for future opportunities and I had family and friends there.

After being on the job for about a year, I was able to serve as a co-anchor/solo anchor on weekends. Shortly thereafter, I was able to fill in as co-anchor on the Morning Show during weekdays; and co-anchor/solo anchor during the 12 Noon Show on weekdays. I was even blessed to fill in as co-anchor for an extended period on the Morning Show, while the main anchor was on maternity leave. For all these blessings, I give God the glory. I know there will always be challenges in life, but I am thrilled that God knows what I need, when I need it. He always comes through right on time. I have learned that when God shows His favor, He does it in a mighty way. I outlined several goals and objectives I had for my life. Sometimes I wondered if they would happen. My mother always told me, "You have to go through to get to. The experience gives you a testimony." I am grateful for the opportunities I have had at CBS Miami and I look forward to God's continued favor in my professional, spiritual, and personal life.

I am currently back and forth between stilettos and high heels when I am anchoring and I usually wear flats when I am reporting. I still pull out my running shoes to get in a good daily workout. I love style and fashion, so it's nothing to see me in low boots or high boots. I love sandals and I also love pumps. I love closed toe shoes and I love open toe shoes. Basically, I have grown into a very diverse person. I believe I am a global citizen and I look forward to traveling to places far and near. I want to be ready and able to walk tall; jump high; and rise to the top of my field. I have journeyed from track shoes to stilettos, experiencing some of life's highs and some of its lows. But, I do know that God continues to go before me and prepare the way. I thank Him for His grace and His mercy and His many blessings.

Part IV

The Shoe Store

CHAPTER 12

All God's Children Got Shoes

Relationships are critical. The first contributor is the only male writer and he describes his relationship between the main characters: Carolyn, Summer, and Lucille. The remaining contributors show how relationships between girls and women can be beautiful. However, they can also be challenging. This chapter shares differing perspectives and distinctive experiences—all presented in hopes of inspiring girls and women to pursue excellence, despite difficulties.

In some cases, these contributors focus on the type of work they have done or continue to do. They consider the relevance of polished shoes; musical shoes; high heels, orthopedic, and grieving shoes. Some discuss career-changing shoes; track shoes; rock climbing shoes; saddle shoes; and combat boots. Still others explore stilettos and tennis shoes; civil servant and cooking shoes. Others, hiking boots; nursing shoes, flats, and shoes with spikes.

No matter their experience, these contributors share some of the lessons they have learned; explain their growth and maturity; and discuss some of the twists and turns along the way.

There is an old spiritual that says, "I got shoes, you got shoes, all God's children got shoes." Enjoy these inspiring shoe stories that are only found in "The Shoe Store."

Views from Polished Shoes

By
Gilbert Knowles

I am Gilbert Alexander Knowles, Jr. Due to my close relationship with the three women on the book cover, I am the only male writer in this book. The author, Carolyn Evaughn Knowles is my wife (35 years); Summer Alexia Knowles, my daughter; and Lucille Brown Floyd, my mother-in-law. Since I can remember, I have always maintained highly polished shoes. I believe shoes tell a lot about their wearers. My semi-obsession with polished shoes can be traced back to my childhood. My mother, a registered nurse, wore all white: uniform, stockings, shoes, and cap (with a black stripe). My contribution to the upkeep of this ensemble was to iron uniforms and polish shoes. I took great pride ensuring there were no wrinkles in her uniform and her shoes were white as snow. Mom's spotless shoes reflected a person that took great pride in everything she did. It had to be done well or not at all.

My strong belief in highly polished shoes also reflects my strong sense of high standards; right and wrong; good and bad; and black and white. However, my life's journey has taught me that uncompromising high standards and beliefs at times lead to major disappointments. Right does not always prevail over wrong; good does not always triumph over bad; and gray often rises out the ashes of black and white. I can attest that although life's dust and grime continually soil one's shoes, God's grace and mercy, time and time again, polishes over the dust and grime as if it never existed. When God polishes our shoes, we are able to walk in the sunshine and in the rain; maneuver the smooth and bumpy roads. You see, God's polish is weather and scratch-resistant.

The early years . . . I was born in Miami to Gilbert and Alice Knowles. Both sides of my family are Bahamian. My older sister is Gilda Alicia Knowles. My father was a maintenance crew supervisor (36 years) for the now defunct Eastern Air Lines and my mother was a registered OBGYN nurse (37 years) at Jackson Memorial Hospital. In the mid 1950's my parents purchased a 2-bedroom (later converted the garage into a 3rd bedroom) one-bath home in Liberty City (a section in Miami); one of the few areas African-Americans could purchase homes. The cost of the home was $9,000.

My early life began in a protective environment that sheltered me from too many real struggles and/or disappointments. My sister and I were initially raised as Catholics, where we regularly went to Mass and attended the church's private school. This all changed when my mother (dad's second wife) was denied the sacrament (divorce not recognized). We left the Catholic Church and became Baptists. I can still remember my submersion into the cold, early morning waters of Virginia Key Beach (at the time the only beach in which African Americans were allowed to swim). Gilda and I left the Catholic private school for public school.

Mom was the first person to join the Drake Memorial Baptist Church on 58th and N.W. 2nd Ave. I became a junior deacon, junior Sunday school superintendent, junior usher, junior choir member, and played the piano for our Baptist Training Union (BTU). My father rarely attended church. I can't remember him attending more than maybe five times throughout my childhood. Forty years later (one week prior to his death) I would lead him to accept Christ as his personal savior. My mother, now also deceased, was always grateful to me for helping lead her husband of 49 ½ years to Christ before he died.

My high school years were more eventful: I was elected president of the prestigious Boy Counselors Club (70-member group of young male leaders/role models); selected as a model for a local formal wear store (this gained me much attention from the ladies at all the high schools); won "Most School Service" senior superlative; named senior class Chaplain; and was an honor student (top 10% of a class of 650). During this protected time of my life, keeping my shoes polished was an easy task. My last two years of high school were some of the greatest years of my life.

Although my father (airlines employee) could get free plane tickets, I did not take my first flight (18 years old) until leaving for Saint Augustine's College (St. Aug) in Raleigh, NC. As I think about it, up until leaving for college, the only other time I left Miami was to visit Saint Augustine, FL—two different saints with the same name.

Enter Carolyn Evaughn Floyd—My experience at Saint Aug was totally outstanding. I thoroughly enjoyed meeting people from all over the United States. The diversity of backgrounds and beliefs opened my eyes to new and different perspectives on almost every topic. I found myself gravitating towards students from South Carolina (especially Charleston). I later determined this gravitation was prompted by their Bahamian flavor. Their accents, love for rice, and forthrightness made me feel right at home. Early in my sophomore year while sitting with friends in the college cafeteria, I got a first glimpse of my future wife. All of the guys (mostly from South Carolina) were making a big deal over this young lady as she passed our table. They all declared that she was one of the finest of this year's freshman crop. Not to be disrespectful, but each year the guys would determine the finest women in the freshman class (we called it crop). They made such a fuss over her that I felt somewhat obliged to say something: "She looks alright."

Since that day in the cafeteria I started observing this beautiful sister. Her name was Carolyn Floyd, a freshman from Charleston, SC. Since many of my friends were from Charleston, I inquired about her. They all gave her high marks for being a very smart young lady. She had recently broken up with her high school boyfriend. I saw an eventual opening, but strongly felt that I should not move too soon.

I was very happy to learn that Carolyn had joined the college's U.S. Army ROTC Program, where I was a sophomore cadet. I guess in today's environment, I would be considered a stalker because I definitely observed her comings and goings. I knew both her class and work-study schedules. She worked on the checkout desk in the college library. I was not a work-study student, so I had total control over my time. All of a sudden, I had a keen interest in reading and studying in the library. Of course I synchronized checking out books with Carolyn's work-study schedule.

As time went on, we got to know each other. One day she told me that I was like a brother and I immediately replied that I had no interest in becoming her brother. We eventually became girlfriend and boyfriend on my birthday, September 16, 1974 (I planned a year earlier that I would ask her to be my girlfriend on my birthday of my junior year). We both flourished over the next two years. I was appointed student representative to the college's board of trustees and at the end of my junior year was elected president of the Student Government Association (SGA) and chosen by my classmates as "Most Likely to Succeed." Carolyn became a member of Delta Sigma Theta Sorority, Inc. and I became a member of Alpha Phi Alpha Fraternity, Inc. Carolyn was later elected "Miss Alpha Phi Alpha" two years in a row and later the student body elected her "Miss Saint Augustine's College," 1977. I also graduated with honors.

As a junior ROTC cadet, Carolyn began receiving a $100 a month stipend. While my ROTC stipend supplemented my spending money I received from home, Carolyn would send all of her stipend home to her mother. I never quite understood why the baby sister of five older brothers had to send money home. My first visit to Charleston better explained why. I remember meeting her mother for the first time. She was very nice. I believe I was able to mask my utter shock when I saw where she lived. Initially, I thought the nicely appointed front house was her family's home until we walked past that house to the dilapidated house in the backyard. Carolyn, her mother, and brother lived in the apartment on the second floor and another family occupied the first floor. After this visit, I loved my Carolyn even more. A beautiful flower had blossomed from very rough soil.

I graduated college and was commissioned an Army Second Lieutenant assigned to Fort Leonard Wood (affectionately known as Fort Lost in the Woods), MO. I loved the military's rules and regulations, officer's honor code, and polished boots. A year later, Carolyn graduated and was commissioned a Second Lieutenant. She requested to be assigned to Fort Lost in the Woods and the Army immediately obliged. Carolyn continued helping her mother by providing a $200 monthly allotment (out of $550 bring home pay). She also aided her mother in purchasing a townhome. Carolyn agreed to marry me with one condition. She would always have to take care of her mother. Due to my naiveté, I thought the five older brothers would also help, thus lessening the financial burden on the newly married couple. This "taking care of mom" pledge would affect us in a big way years later.

We married a year later, August 12, 1978 in a military wedding with over 300 guests. I started calling Carolyn's mom, Li'l Lady (she is about 4' 10), a name that most people call her today. We started sending Li'l Lady $250 a month and Alice, the woman who helped raise Carolyn, $100. Carolyn and I were soon assigned to Korea, a beautiful country with a great culture. After a year in Korea, we were assigned to Atlanta.

Enter Summer Alexia Knowles—Carolyn and I loved Atlanta. We purchased our first home and after 3 ½ years of marriage decided to have a child. Carolyn was very cute and petite throughout the pregnancy. As the time neared, we became very anxious. We had a false alarm, thinking it was time to be admitted. However, the doctor indicated that was not the case. So, we returned home. We sent for Li'l Lady to spend a couple of weeks before and after the baby arrived. On a snow filled Saturday afternoon Carolyn alerted me that it was time. We thought the baby was on its way on Saturday evening. I selfishly thought the birth would happen prior to Sunday's Super Bowl XVI (San Francisco 49ers vs. Cincinnati Bengals). Saturday evening came, but no baby. Sunday morning came, still no baby. Game time came, still no baby. I was smart enough to not attempt to turn on the TV to catch a glimpse of the game. Carolyn was not a happy camper during the labor process. She wanted— no—DEMANDED my undivided attention. It also seemed as if the baby also wanted my full attention.

At about 7 p.m., the doctor, utilizing a plastic hook instrument, induced labor. I recall the gush of amniotic fluid fully soaking the bed. Everyone immediately started moving Carolyn to the operating room to deliver the baby. I was just standing there until the nurse guided me to a room to put on hospital scrubs. It took some time to find scrubs large enough to fit. I remember hanging around the sink outside the operating room to scrub up, like I saw the doctors do on TV. The doctor laughed saying I did not have to wash up.

On Sunday, January 24, 1982, at 8:15 p.m. (the Super Bowl game had ended), Summer Alexia Knowles was born into this world. She was twenty one inches long and weighed seven pounds and nine ounces. Although I am told that baby's eyes are not focused at birth, I remember Summer staring into my eyes as if to say, "I'm here!" I now tease Summer about how her spectacular entrance, after many hours of labor and my missing the Super Bowl game, gained everyone's full attention.

Summer's addition to the Knowles team completely changed our lives. We had to get used to having her around. One day we got almost half way home before we realized we had not picked up Summer from the child care center. The center was located at the Army post. Carolyn and I would spend most of our lunch times visiting and taking her outside in the stroller.

After a couple of weeks, Li'l Lady went home and my mom, dad, and sister came to visit. Summer was the first grandchild on my side of the family. Our next assignment was a brief six months of school in Indianapolis, IN, and then on to Dallas/Fort Worth. Carolyn was an ROTC instructor at Texas Christian University-Fort Worth, and I was an Adjutant for the Dallas Recruiting Battalion. We purchased a beautiful home in North Richland Hills, a northern suburb of Fort Worth. I later had an opportunity to become the Waco Recruiting Commander. I was responsible for forty five recruiters at stations in Waco, Temple, Corsicana, Tyler, Palestine, and Killeen, TX. I had to move over 100 miles away from home and rent an apartment.

The stressors of financing two separate households, meeting recruiting quotas, having Carolyn take care of Summer alone resulted in the worst years of our marriage. I would come home on weekends tired. However, Carolyn after working and taking care of Summer alone, was tired as well. The Texas dust continually soiled my polished shoes. I asked God to deliver us from this environment. I had never experienced true racism until I lived in Texas. Eventually, we would be happy to view Texas in our car's rear view mirror as we left for our next assignment in Germany. Years later, I would have my first "Driving While Black" experience right outside of Dallas.

Enter Lucille Brown Floyd (aka Li'l Lady) . . . Our assignment to Germany proved to be our very best. We both flourished in our careers and were quite happy. I was the Director of Community Activities for 18,000 soldiers and their families. My staff of almost 300 supported this community through military clubs, child care centers, libraries, gymnasiums, sports programs, recreation centers, and alcohol and substance abuse centers. This position was the best job I had in the Army. Carolyn was commander of a Data Processing Unit. Summer was enrolled in day care. We met new friends and learned about a totally different culture.

Combat alerts (periodic early morning tests for combat readiness) presented a problem for us. We had to make arrangements to leave Summer with friends during the alerts. We decided to ask Li'l Lady if she would come live with us in Europe. This proved to be a win-win situation. Li'l Lady would no longer have to pay for the mortgage (her baby son and family would move in and pay rent), utilities, food and clothing. We also provided her with a small salary. I'll never forget picking up Li'l Lady at the airport in Frankfurt, Germany. All I could see off in the distance was a little lady with suitcases (tied with ropes) leaking water (frozen collard greens and black eyed peas). One of the first things I bought Li'l Lady was new luggage. She still kept the old luggage (her don't throw anything away mentality prevails to this very day).

Li'l Lady living with us in tight quarters became quite an adjustment for us all. She can be very strong in her opinions and perspectives believing others should always think her way. Of course, that would cause major conflict. Li'l Lady believed that one should not iron on Sunday. I would find myself sneaking to iron my shirt on Sunday morning for church. Lord help you, if she caught you. After a while, I determined that I would no longer sneak and iron on Sunday mornings; this was my house. She started crying one Sunday morning after I sternly told her to show me in the Bible where thou shalt not iron on Sunday!

Before coming to Germany, Li'l Lady would rarely buy clothes from a store. Historically, she made all of her clothes and hats. However, after spending 2 ½ years in Germany, we bought her the latest fashions in clothes and hats. Li'l Lady, in her mid-fifties, had rarely traveled outside of Charleston. However, she was now living in Germany with travels to France, Spain, Italy, Austria, Netherlands, Belgium, and Luxembourg. We were in Germany when the Berlin Wall fell. We will always treasure our time there.

The only regret of our European experience was that Summer was too young to appreciate our travels. I remember us being at the foot of the Eiffel Tower, telling Summer to look up. Her major concern was if we were going to McDonalds for lunch. While in Germany, I was selected to attend the prestigious U.S. Army Command and General Staff College, Fort Leavenworth, KS. This resident course would last one year. Carolyn was assigned to the office of the commanding general.

Li'l Lady continued living with us in Fort Leavenworth. We joined an off-post Baptist Church that we all loved. The Independent Baptist Church ordained me as a deacon. Carolyn and I jointly taught a very popular and well attended Sunday school class. During this time, I was in the best physical shape of my life. I would wake up early each morning and run five miles with a group of fellow officers. I felt amazingly well all that time! During this time my polished shoes took second place to my running shoes. Li'l Lady developed close friendships with people her age in Fort Leavenworth. We were always trying to find her a new beau, but that never happened.

Upon graduation, I was selected to remain in Leavenworth as a Leadership Instructor at the college. That year I made the promotion list to Lieutenant Colonel, to be promoted within the next 10-11 months. During that time, a requirement for a temporary assignment came available for an Army Lieutenant Colonel in support of Operation Restore Hope-Somalia. Although I had not yet been promoted from Major to Lieutenant Colonel, they "frocked" (authorization to wear the next rank) me and sent me to Mogadishu.

My five-month stint in Somalia was quite challenging. I never received the canvass boots made for the sandy environment. Therefore, the Somalian dust would cover my polished black boots. Every night, I would still polish my black boots, although they would be covered by sand within minutes. I was one of only two Army officers assigned to work with a very large contingent of Marines. Due to an illness, my Marine colonel boss had to return to the states. I was named his replacement. I was now a Major, frocked as a Lieutenant Colonel, assuming a Colonel's position. I worked very well with the Marines. We departed Somalia and flew into Andrews Air Force Base, where we were driven directly to the White House. We met President Bill Clinton and Vice President Al Gore right outside of the oval office and marched behind President Clinton as he held a press conference on the White House lawn.

Upon my return to Fort Leavenworth, I was named Director of all Department of the Army Civilian Workforce Leadership Training, a job I tremendously enjoyed. During this time, Carolyn decided to retire from the Army. As my tour in Leavenworth came to an end, there was talk of me being assigned to San Francisco as Postal Commander for the Pacific Command. However, word came that the president of my alma mater, Dr. Prezell Robinson, had requested me by name to become the Professor of Military Science (PMS) of the U.S. Army ROTC at St. Aug and Shaw University. The Army immediately obliged and assigned me to Raleigh, NC. Being assigned as the first St. Aug alumni to become PMS was a great honor. I couldn't believe eighteen years later, I would be leading the very same program that produced me.

Carolyn was hired as a professor in the college's business division. Summer was happy entering middle school. And, Li'l Lady was happy meeting friends her own age. A couple of years later, Li'l Lady moved back to Charleston to help take care of a grandson. Although I was quite confident I would make the Colonel's promotion list in the next few years, I started thinking of retiring instead at 20 years. The new college president (Dr. Robinson retired a year after I arrived), Dr. Bernard Franklin, heard about my considering retirement and offered me the position of Dean of Students. He was impressed with my ability to make strong connections with the students. Summer had just entered ninth grade and Carolyn was happy teaching. I chose my family's happiness and stability over continuing in the military. Therefore, I retired on a Monday and started as Dean of Students on Tuesday. I later became Vice President of Student Affairs.

Summer became quite a sports celebrity in Raleigh. In her tenth-grade year, she won three state track championships (100 meters, 200 meters and 100 meter hurdles). She also won the 100—meter hurdles competing against young women representing eastern seaboard states from Boston to Miami. She appeared in the Raleigh newspaper quite a few times. One day while jokingly playing football with a friend, she tore her ACL and had to have surgery. Unfortunately, she was never the same. At an early age, Summer learned a valuable life lesson in experiencing how a person can go from hero to zero in the public's eyes in a short period of time. Summer still received scholarship offers from Seton Hall, Clemson, and University of

North Carolina-Chapel Hill. The Chapel Hill coach even visited our home to sign Summer. Carolyn and I told him about how her injury had impacted her running ability. He still offered her a full, 4-year track scholarship to attend Chapel Hill, one of the top three public universities in the country and in the top 25 of all American colleges and universities. Summer loved her experience at Chapel Hill and wants her kids to attend one day. She also pledged Carolyn's sorority becoming a member of Delta Sigma Theta Sorority, Inc. Carolyn was able to pin her daughter at the intake ceremony.

Carolyn and I moved from Raleigh to northern Virginia during Summer's sophomore year. We both worked at the United Negro College Fund Special Programs Corporation (UNCFSP). We purchased a beautiful home in a gated community in Haymarket, VA (forty miles west of Washington, D.C.). After a couple of years, Carolyn got a job as a GS-15 civil servant. I remained and eventually became the Director of the Division of Community and Education. We joined Alfred Street Baptist Church in Alexandria, VA, where I serve as a deacon and Carolyn sings in the Trinity Choir.

Summer graduated from the University of North Carolina at Chapel Hill with a degree in Broadcast Journalism. Her career thus far: Assistant Producer at NBC, Charlotte, NC; TV news reporter, FOX, Charlottesville, VA; TV news reporter, FOX, St. Louis, MO; TV news reporter, CBS, West Palm Beach, FL; TV news anchor/reporter, CBS, Shreveport, LA; TV news reporter (also selected as a fill-in morning news co-anchor), CBS Miami, FL.

My dad died in November, 2000. My mom died almost 10 years later on January 23, 2010, a day before Summer's birthday. Over the years, I traveled back and forth from Virginia to Miami to see about mom. This beautiful, strong, proud, loving, caring, and extremely independent mother was a blessing to so many people. My beloved aunt, Alva J. McLeod (mom's baby sister and now the matriarch of our family), Summer, and I were at mom's bedside when the nurse announced, "She is gone." We were playing mom's favorite gospel songs and praying as she took her last breath. Mom died at home like she always wanted. I miss her so much and think of her every day. I will always remember that my Mom did not die alone!

Re-enter Lucille Brown Floyd (Li'l Lady)—Life was great for Carolyn and me. I even wrote a book, *Help Them Pull Their Pants Up . . . How Mentors and Communities Can Empower Young African American Men* and started a business, KNOWLES What To Do Mentoring Solutions, which facilitates Black male initiatives at churches and Historically Black Colleges and Universities. Over the years, we would send for Li'l Lady to spend six weeks with us during the summer months. In the course of her last visit, we noticed how age was taking its toll on her and decided it was time for her to move in with us in Virginia.

At this time, Li'l Lady was eighty six years old and somewhat frail. We moved her into our Jack and Jill suite, with two bedrooms (one converted into a day room), separated by a full bathroom. We found some excellent doctors; an African-American female specializing in geriatrics and an African-American female optometrist. Both doctors treat her with the utmost care and respect. At the end of each visit, Li'l Lady requests that we all hold hands and pray.

We enrolled Li'l Lady in a senior center that picks her up twice a week from 8 a.m. to 2 p.m. The center has a multitude of activities (e.g. arts and crafts, senior exercises, playing cards, bridge, etc.). Unfortunately, Li'l Lady chooses not to participate. She just sits and watches others and uses her cell phone to call people in South Carolina. Li'l Lady is almost ninety years old and has outlived most of her friends.

Musings of a Caregiver—Carolyn works in DC and has an average daily commute (roundtrip) of almost four hours. I am trying to work the business from home. Therefore, I have become Li'l Lady's major caregiver. I often times remember Carolyn's one condition to marrying me, "I will always have to take care of my mother." At the naïve age of 23, I thought things would eventually get better. I just knew that Li'l Lady would eventually become more financially independent. However, that never happened. I have to remain in continual prayer and focus on helping my wife of over thirty five years take care of her mother, and not focus on people or things that can cause me to get frustrated and/or full of resentment.

All who know our situation say that I have spoiled Li'l Lady. I prepare a hot breakfast for her every morning; manage her prescriptions; prepare a lunch bag twice a week before the bus picks her up for the senior center, as well as handle many of her other needs and desires. You see, Li'l Lady loves to be coddled. Therefore, a nice lady at the center has adopted her and takes care of her while she is there. Because Li'l Lady doesn't eat much, I fix her a snack with things I know she likes.

Li'l Lady does not seem to realize it, but she complains about everything. If it's not her eyes, it's her hips; if it's not her hips, it's her feet; if it's not her feet, it's her fingers; if it's not her fingers, it's her back; if it's not her back, she feels dizzy. She tells people that she doesn't go anywhere and doesn't talk to anyone. Carolyn and I have decided to no longer allow those negative comments to bother us, because Li'l Lady goes to the senior center twice a week. Carolyn takes her to choir rehearsal sometimes, and she goes to church almost every Sunday. Our church's Trinity Choir has even named her "Choir Mother." Li'l Lady periodically sings a solo with the eighty to ninety-member Trinity Choir backing her up.

Most weekdays Carolyn, after a hard day's work and long commute, ensures she sits with Li'l Lady for dinner. On Saturdays she takes Li'l Lady shopping at Walmart or the local grocery store. She tries to wash, grease, and braid her hair weekly. Li'l Lady requires so much attention. She interrupts me at least twenty five to thirty times a day while I am trying to work from our home office.

We purchased a stair lift that she rarely uses; pay for an emergency necklace that she rarely wears; pay for cell phone service that she wants, but cannot seem to operate (although we have eight of her closest supporters on speed dial); and we even pay for an additional cable box for her bedroom, so that she can get the gospel channel.

Statistics prove that almost 40% of caregivers die prior to the person(s) they are taking care of. I have found my health declining and must make a hard decision to take better care of myself—make myself a priority. Although we are struggling with Li'l Lady, we know it is the right thing to do. It is the CHRIST—like thing to do.

In the end—Although caregiving and other life challenges can be strains on a marriage, Carolyn and I are in this relationship until death do us part. Summer continues to flourish as she experiences life to the fullest. The strength of our love and commitment endures. My polished shoes will continue to get soiled, scratched, scraped, and worn. God's word provides the polish; God's love provides the repair; and God's mercy provides new shoes when needed.

As I return to our situation, my prayer is that I return rejoicing, knowing that God is the strength of my life and He will continue to bless me and our family in a mighty way.

And we know that all things work together
for good to them that love God, to
them who are called according to his
purpose.

Romans 8:23 (KJV)

Joyce's Musical Shoes

By
Dr. Joyce Garrett

I began taking piano lessons at six years of age. I don't remember this, but my aunt, who served as my guardian, remarked that she noticed I showed early signs of having musical talent. Although I never liked to practice on the old, out-of-tune, upright piano in the living room, I continued my weekly lessons until I graduated from high school.

Somewhere around the third or fourth grade, I knew that I wanted to be a choir director. I had gone to a concert at our local segregated high school, and heard these wonderful, rich voices of the upperclassmen singing spirituals and classical choruses. I recognized some of this music from the selections I played during my piano lessons. The graded, John Thompson piano method books included many piano transcriptions of classical melodies. My family, striving to be the first generation to move into the middle class, encouraged my love of this music because they frowned upon the playing of jazz or the new music called, "rock and roll."

I got my chance to work with a real choir at the age of twelve, when I began serving as pianist for a rural youth gospel choir. One of my aunts managed the group. I enjoyed the car rides where the driver would pick up singers for rehearsal then transport everyone back home afterwards. I became fascinated with learning about the families who lived in the homes that dotted the length of the dirt roads. I greatly enjoyed participating in choir rehearsal. It was an avenue for social interaction with my peers who were growing up "in the country." At the same time, it presented me with an opportunity to learn leadership and service. During the summer months I would work at my aunt's farm in the tobacco barn, in rural Dover, NC. During the day, we could listen only to traditional quartet music on the radio.

During my junior year in high school, my home church, the Antioch Free Will Baptist Church, in Kinston, NC, organized the Youth Church, a service on the second Sunday of each month where the children and youth participated in all facets of the worship service, except preaching. I served as the youth choir accompanist and continued to model the leadership skills I learned in my high school choir. It was clearly evident that I loved singing in and working with choirs.

Once I enrolled in Bennett College, a small, but prestigious women's college in Greensboro, NC, I organized a small gospel group due to the fact that Gospel music was not included in the curriculum of study for music majors. This was considered revolutionary, at the time, because Gospel music was not considered music for educated folks. There was something about the Gospel classics that I loved. To me, there were 360 degrees of music and I wanted to appreciate and assign value to every one of them, not just classical music. The key was to present all music with excellence and refinement. That philosophy of musical inclusion with excellence became the rock upon which my career as a teacher and church musician would be later established.

My musical shoes became multi-colored, coated with a flexible and altruistic fabric, with hard-surfaced leather bottoms made to last for the journey. After I began teaching in the Washington, DC public school system, my musical shoes were used not only to serve as teacher, director, or accompanist, they stretched to visit my students' homes, frequently to places of neglect, abuse, and family dysfunction. Sometimes, I needed to purchase food for a hungry teen, who had not eaten all day at school. Other times, shoes were needed to drive to a department store to purchase a winter coat or school supplies. My shoes stepped between students who had never learned methods of conflict resolution and were intent upon fighting each other. My shoes stood outside the school waiting for late parents to pick up a child from an evening performance. These shoes sat motionless in the car when students kept stalling because they did not want to go home after school. My shoes walked briskly to return to my car after visiting a former student in a slum apartment building where gun shots had rung out just hours earlier.

However, along the way, many miracles happened! In 1988, following a triumphant return from Vienna, Austria, where my Eastern High School Choir won second place at the International Youth and Music Festival, I was invited by then-President Ronald Reagan to present a concert in the East Room of the White House. This singular honor was followed in quick succession by appearances on NBC-TV's "Today Show" and numerous nationally-televised specials including "Christmas in Washington" (NBC-TV) and the "Kennedy Center Honors" (CBS-TV). Eastern singers became the choir of choice for many of the world's top artists, soon supplying background vocals for Diana Ross, Stevie Wonder, Patti Labelle, James Taylor, Natalie Cole, Aretha Franklin, Johnny Mathis, Barry Manilow, Carole King, Roberta Flack, Gloria Estefan, and many others. Incredible opportunities unfolded! We performed at the Lincoln Memorial for President Clinton's Inaugural Eve Concert in 1997; I directed a choir that provided background vocals for President Clinton as he ushered in the new Millennium from the steps of the Lincoln Memorial; I later prepared two large choirs to perform at President Obama's historic Inauguration Gala Concert in 2008 under the revered gaze of the Lincoln Memorial. My shoes had taken gigantic leaps of awe and wonder.

International soil dusted my leather soles in France (Paris and Normandy), Germany, Austria, and the Netherlands where the Eastern Choir was invited to sing. My shoes had to demonstrate leadership and artistic competence in these majestic concert halls and European cathedrals. I learned how to prepare my music thoroughly, and then walk confidently into each new and blessed opportunity, no matter how frightened I might have been. I am a witness that it's possible for shoes to go from a tobacco barn to the White House . . . in one generation!

As director of the United States Naval Academy Gospel Choir from 1990-2006, my shoes walked down the long, hallowed halls of the college; they marched proudly down the aisles of the glorious chapel on several Sunday mornings and touched the soil of numerous American cities as we honored God and country in some amazing ways. The same feet, but oh, such different shoes, traveled to Annapolis, MD, to one of our country's most prestigious colleges, where I conducted a choir of premier national scholars of proven and tried character.

There have been three pairs of shoes that I have worn most—school choir shoes, church choir shoes, and family shoes. Since that first choir as a twelve year old child, I have continued to lead and direct church choirs to this present time. Church shoes have their own story to tell: a tale of faithfulness, dedication, and commitment. On the other hand, school shoes many times revealed an edge of caution and low expectations. Church shoes are shod with the gospel of peace. They have a mandate of purposeful action and must always "go" somewhere: to choir rehearsal, to a funeral to comfort a grieving family; to worship services that are formal or informal; to committee and staff meetings that are too numerous to count; to pedals of the gospel and rhythm-infused Hammond organ or the majestic and powerful Rodgers pipe organ; and to towns and cities nearby and afar—wherever the gospel is shared with other believers.

As a wife and mother of two children, a special pair of family shoes became my priority. However, as I look back it seems as though at times I put on my school and counselor shoes more firmly than my family shoes. Thankfully, my loving family somehow understood that I was passionate about helping others become all that they could be. Today, my husband and adult children wear even larger pairs of my old multi-colored shoes with the flexible and caring shoe laces. I smile when I see that these shoes actually fit them well!

How did my musical shoes turn halting, baby steps into a full-fledged marathon? The answer: the love of music and the love of people. This glue held together people and situations. Music's majestic and transforming power has been the hallmark of my life. Providing a means of self-expression, it led under-privileged youth to a higher state of self-esteem and character development. No matter what the environment, music taught teamwork and discipline. Whether from an impoverished community or from an affluent background, my students learned that excellence requires study and practice. They discovered that musical discipline could lead to success in life. There was value in sustained effort towards high achievement. I realize that these musical shoes stood at attention with pride while witnessing college graduations of students who had overcome tremendous odds to earn college degrees. Now their own shoes can take them to a life of limitless opportunities. For this, I am grateful.

My prayer is that my multi-faceted musical shoes have taught my singers and family members to perform anywhere in the world with fearless effort and world-class standards of excellence. May their shoes, born out of life's triumphs and challenges, take them to a world of amazing and unlimited experiences as they walk in the beauty and glory of living on this amazing planet earth.

Gale's High Heels, Orthopedic, and Bereavement Shoes

By
Ms. Gale Rolle

My name is Gale Leonard Rolle. I am African American and a child of God who has been wonderfully and perfectly made in His image. God thought so much of me that He must have said, "Now this one will stand 5 feet 9 ½ inches tall with lanky legs, knock knees, and not be curvaceous at all. However, she will love people. Color, ethnicity, and gender will not matter to her, as long as her color, ethnicity, and gender do not matter to them."

Family and friends have said that I am funny and have the gift of gab. They have also said that I am a giver, so much so that I have taken a ring, watch, shoes, and yes—even the wig off my head—and given it to someone who needed it. I would say, "take it, it's yours, enjoy." I am a good listener and have been told by a friend that my spiritual gift is encouragement. Being a tall woman, I have one shoulder on which you can lean and rest your head. That would be the left one. I had rotator cuff repair surgery on the right shoulder, so don't even think about leaning on that side.

I am blessed and highly favored by God. I was blessed to have a mother who instilled in me good morals and values. I was raised by a single parent who knew how to take one chicken, two cans of vegetables, and two cups of rice to make a scrumptious dinner for the family. Mom was the neighborhood hairdresser who fed the hungry and gave to the needy. Growing up in Georgia, my mom's hands helped plow the fields, pick cotton, string tobacco, and maintain the family's large garden. Her hands showed signs of age but they were so gentle that when she stroked my arms, hair, neck, and back, they felt like silk. She was so sweet and gentle and had a kind spirit. When she looked into my eyes the way only a mother could, she was silently saying, "Baby it's gonna be alright." She had such a loving, motherly smile that gave me the reassurance, which said, "You are my daughter whom I love." Her voice was so angelic without the benefits of having a voice coach. When Mom sang, her voice turned everyone's head.

My mom and I looked so much alike that even our hands and fingernails were shaped the same. My mom was diagnosed with dementia several years ago. Dementia is when you lose your mental skills and have memory loss. So, for the last six or seven years, my beautiful, loving jewel of a mother no longer recognized me. However, she has kept a song in her heart. Mom and I were tight. We spent just about every Monday together. I called our times together, "Mondays with Mom." We were like girlfriends. I'd push her in the wheel chair and we'd go to Target, Walmart, J.C. Penney, Red Lobster, Piccadilly's Cafeteria, and International House of Pancakes. I would put in a CD and we'd sing and sing. She and I both would put on our sunglasses and she once asked, "Why do I need sunglasses?" I answered, "So we can be cool like that." We laughed out loud!

Mom became ill so suddenly, so unexpectedly! On that very sad day of April 6, 2013, God allowed me one more time to sing to mom. As

I folded her hand into mine, I pressed my cheek against her cheek, and I sang our favorite song. This time it was not a duet. It was a solo. I am not sure who the writer is but one stanza of the song is below:

> God has smiled on me,
> He has set me free.
> God has smiled on me,
> He's been good to me.

The Bible says our lives are like a vapor; like a mist. And, like a mist, mom was gone.

It's a blessing to have a good family and solid friends. I have four good friends and one best friend. An African Proverb says, "If you find a friend, hold him or her in the palm of your hand." This is true. Don't let go of them.

I am so grateful and thankful for my two handsome sons—Jamaal and Rashad. They help "keep the pep" in my step. They have date night with me. We go to dinner and a movie. And yes at fifty eight years old, I put on my four-inch heels and strut my stuff with them! We've gone several times to South Beach. When I see different places and people, who seem very strange, my sons say, "It's just strange to you ma—It's exposure." Yet, I perceive South Beach as a place that's hot, with limited parking, and very expensive outdoor dining. However, I take it all in—and for that I am grateful.

It gives me great joy to say that I was raised in Liberty City, FL, in the James E. Scott Housing Project. During this period, there really was a "village;" a loving neighborhood with lots of love, sharing, and caring.

In this village, the elders gave love as well as chastisement. They told your parents on you when you were caught doing something wrong. There were block parties where everybody came together. Each family brought something to the party: conch fritters, conch salad, potato salad, pigeon peas and rice, barbecue chicken, barbecue ribs, pickled pigs' feet, etc. We blasted the music of the era: Chaka Kahn, Graham Central Station, Sly and the Family Stone, Marvin Gaye, Curtis Mayfield, and Gladys Knight and the Pips. We loved hoola-hooping, skating, and riding bicycles. These memories will be forever embedded in my heart. So, don't believe the "hype" that the housing project was nothing but a "ghetto" with a whole lot of misfits. I beg to differ. Of course we had several who went astray, but we had a whole lot more who have made positive impacts on society.

As I continue to reflect, I can remember the following conversation between my beloved Kenny Rolle (aka Falfa) and me. He would approach my mom's front door and call out, "Slim, you wanna go to the movies or the park? Or, do you wanna go to China Man Joe's Store? Better yet, let's go to Mr. Mutt's Store and buy a pig's foot, hot sausage, or a Nehi Soda." My response was, "Do you have any money?" He would say, "Yeah, I have a dollar." I'd say, "Sounds good to me. I'll be out as soon as I put on my shoes."

Falfa was my best friend. He was 6 feet 5 inches tall and about 180 pounds. He had a bad afro, with the prettiest white teeth and a smile as wide as Twenty Second Avenue. He also had a little swag. Falfa and I confided in each other, sharing our most precious secrets. He was so comical and always having something funny to say. He once told me, "You know you have nice breasts, but you are knock-kneed and your butt is so flat." I laughed because it was true. He also said, "I think you are pretty." He was right about that, too.

Sometimes, Falfa would call me dizzy. Usually, I would answer. However, one day I said, "If you call me dizzy one more time, don't ever come back to 2154 N.W. 69th Lane." Of course calling me by that name stopped immediately.

On Saturdays, Falfa, our friend Magalean, and I would catch the #21 bus to Northside Movie Theatre. Magalean and I would dress up because you never knew who you might see or meet at the theatre. (Of course Falfa chose not to do so.)

I would put on my hot pants, popcorn blouse, fish net stockings, and some cute high heels. I would think to myself, "Look out world, here comes Slim." One particular Saturday, after returning from seeing "Shaft in South Africa," Falfa told Magalean that he was in love with me! Magalean came to my Mom's house and relayed that startling message. I literally rolled off my Mom's plastic covered couch onto our white shag carpet. Oh no, not Falfa! I see him as a brother. He is my best friend. I said, "That won't work. How could he betray me like that?" As a matter of fact, I decided to stop speaking to him.

I explained Falfa's betrayal to my Mom. To my surprise, she said, "I think you two would make a great couple and he is quite handsome." This was not the answer I expected. I was still upset with Falfa, but I gradually began to speak to him again. I also began to see him in a new light. I noticed that he really was quite handsome and he knew how to make me blush.

Wake up Gale! What happened to brotherly and sisterly love? Well, it went right out the window. As he was smiling, Falfa said to me, "If you don't wanna be my girlfriend, I'd date your Mom because you look just like her."

After seven years as best friends and six years of dating, we became one on June 10, 1979. God blessed us with two wonderful sons. Jamaal looks just like me and Rashad is the spitting image of Falfa.

I loved my Kenny so much. He was no longer Falfa to me. I was blessed to have been married to him for almost 30 years. He meant a lot to me. He was my King; my soul mate; and a mighty warrior.

In our intimate times, I called him "Honey Bun" and he called me "Slim" and "Babe."

Kenny was passionate about the plight of Black people. He was the activist and warrior who stood up for what was right. We participated in rallies and marches that were local as well as out of town. Kenny worked in the Miami Dade County Public School System for 30 years. His passion for all children motivated him to get up every morning and rally for the kids.

On October 28, 2008, Kenny left all of us. His body was rife of metastasized cancer. I had questions for God! "God, what happened to our plans of growing old together, buying a Winnebago and traveling across the country, spoiling the grand kids, meeting the mail man at the mailbox on the third of each month for our pension checks?" My idea of happily ever after had come too soon. Death wasn't a part of the plans. I felt blindsided! The sole of my feet had to be adjusted for a solo walk!

Some people didn't know how to comfort me. They would say, "Where is your faith? God makes no mistakes. You are young and can get someone else." I would say, "Woe unto you for you still have your man—now leave me alone!"

The year 2008 was one of death, trials, and tribulations. Then, in 2010, I was laid off from the U.S. Postal Services, after 28 years. What I have learned from the death of my king is that life can really be short and every day isn't bright and sunny. People grieve differently and that's alright. I have chosen to not allow family or friends to box me in about how I should grieve or for how long. With the passing of my husband and my jewel of a mother, I have learned to take life one day at a time. My son gave me a tee shirt that said, "Just Live." I love it and I choose to do just that. While I am still here, I choose to continue "leaning forward."

In the fifth year of Kenny's passing, I visited Ghana, West Africa, where the dungeons of slavery still provoke feelings of utter despair. It represents the place of our Black holocaust. Daily, I saw people moving about selling their goods—not from cars, but on foot. I saw a huge lack of bare necessities in 2013. Images of people struggling to live touched my soul to tears, yet they seemed satisfied.

Children showed much gratitude for educational items, such as pencils, pens, erasers, and reading literature. Things that American children take for granted were really valued. In honor of Kenny's love for children, I distributed pouches filled with school supplies.

I visited five of the ten regions of Ghana. These were actual villages where people lived primitive lifestyles and livestock roamed the roads. I saw women carry children tied to their bodies, while they balanced very large containers on their heads—never missing a beat—in stealth determination to work and feed their families. I also saw men trying to earn money by selling their goods.

During a ninety-minute rain forest walk, I sensed a total cleansing of my soul as the torrential rain washed away layers of anxiety and grief. I have never felt so awakened by such a soaking wet experience. It was the glory of God. Africa has not seen the last of me. It was not just a trip. It was an experience that I will always remember. I saw, learned, and felt connected to Africa—the peace of mankind's beginning.

In my present state I have purchased several pairs of really cute orthopedic sandals. I take walks and I also practice yoga. I am thankful for the rain. Without it, nothing lives. Although I don't like to drive in it, I like the look and sound of it. Rain puts me in a "serene state" and I am thankful for that "peace of mind."

I like to sit on my patio and feed peanuts to the blue jays and blackbirds. I watch them, as they watch me. At the right moment, they swoop down and pick up the peanuts. I watch them crack open the nuts and eat them. I also feed them bread and watch, as they quickly gravitate towards it. I feel really good about feeding the birds that neither reap nor sow, yet God provides for them.

In the trunk of my car I have a folding chair and a beach towel. I like to be prepared to spontaneously stop at either location to walk or contemplate the beauty of the water, as I reflect or meditate with my feet in the grass. How relaxing!

From my soul to my sole, life has transformed me into a woman who wishes for peace in the family, community, and world. The 50th anniversary of the March on Washington occurred in 2013. My legacy embodies some of the same values for which Martin Luther King fought and died. We can't have a peaceful world without peace in the family. My heart's desire is for my family to remain united and rooted in the love of God. We must continue with the struggle to be our brother's keeper; to move closer to a higher level of justice and equality; and to gain a better awareness of our history.

Let the legacy of Gale Leonard Rolle, aka "Slim," be that she is a peacekeeper, lover of family, and devoted mother. Life returns to us whatever we invest. Therefore, we must dream big and never give up. We must make a difference, no matter how small or large. We must slow down, live, and enjoy life.

Jeremiah 29: 11-13 (KJV) says, "For I know the thoughts I think toward you, saith the Lord, thoughts of peace, and not of evil, to give you an expected end. Then shall ye call upon me, and ye shall go and pray unto me, and I will hearken unto you. And ye shall seek me, and find me, when ye shall search for me with all your heart."

Everyone knows the author of this book as Carolyn. We met through our husbands more than 30 years ago. I called her Carol until August of 2008, right before the passing of my husband. One day he said to me, "Her name is not Carol." I said, "Really? Well she never corrected me, so I'll just stick with Carol, if that is okay with you, Mr. Rolle!" We also call each other "my Thugetta," which is a special name that only she and I can call each other.

Carol has been my mentor for twelve years. I count it an honor, as well as a blessing, to have been asked to be a part of this project. My friend and mentor, know that your good deeds, hard work, love for God, Gilbert, and Summer; and your care for your mom has not gone unnoticed. For in due season, you will reap if you faint not. The best is yet to come.

Leaning Forward!

Delisia's Career Changing Shoes

By
Dr. Delisia R. Matthews

I am Delisia R. Matthews. First and foremost, I am God's masterpiece. I am his masterpiece because I am made in his image. Ephesians 2:10 (KJV) states, "For we are His workmanship, created in Christ Jesus unto good works, which God hath before ordained that we should walk in them." Thus, because I am made in His image, I have a responsibility to realize the purpose He has for me, and a duty to fulfill the good works He has ordained me to complete. Secondly, I am enthusiastic. I approach life with optimism and passion. While each day may not be perfect, and trials and tribulations are evident, I have control over how I deal with my struggles. I choose to approach them with hope and positivity. Thirdly, I am imperfect. I am human. Thus, I make mistakes. However, I learn and grow from them. Each mistake is an opportunity to expand my perspective and gain wisdom. Lastly, I am an encourager. God has given me a gift to inspire others to see the beauty and talents within them. Currently, I use this gift in the classroom as a professor. I strive to show my students that there are no limits to what they can accomplish. Their road to success will not be easy; it will take hard work and perseverance. I help them realize their dreams through first assisting them to realize their talents and skills.

I am blessed in so many ways. I am blessed because I was raised in a family that taught me how imperative it is to have a relationship with Christ. Their teachings and examples made an impression on me that have served me well. I am also blessed because I have family and friends who sincerely love me—flaws and all. They allow me to be vulnerable and they share in my joys and successes. Most importantly, they pray for me. Why am I blessed? I am blessed because I am a child of God—plain and simple.

"If the Shoe Doesn't Fit . . . Change the Shoe"

I have always loved fashion. Even as a child, I was intrigued by how various clothing patterns and designs could help an individual express himself or herself. I considered fashion to be wearable art. Even with this passion for fashion, I never truly thought I could make a career out of it. Thus, I pursued marketing, my second passion. I worked for several Fortune 500 companies in corporate marketing over a number of years. All of my experiences were fulfilling and successful. However, there was something that still never quite "fit." I missed the artistry and creativity of fashion and felt within my heart that my calling was different. In other words, the "shoe" I wore didn't "fit." I decided to find my own truth and "change my shoes" for a better "fit." Although my decision was unconventional, I decided to leave my corporate job and pursue career in retail and fashion with Nordstrom. Many people did not support my decision. In fact, most people shared openly with me how they thought I would soon regret my decision. However, that could not have been further away from the truth. I never felt more in my element! Within weeks, I was connecting with customers and providing my styling advice successfully. Weeks after that, I had already developed a client book of customers who specifically came into the department to shop with me. A few months later, I was given the honor of Nordstrom Customer All-Star, which is one of the highest honors within the company. Obviously, I had found the "shoe that fit" . . . and months after, evidence that the "shoe fit" came to fruition when I was asked to move to Charlotte, NC as a department manager to help open a brand new Nordstrom store. Thank God I had the guts to not get stuck being complacent in "shoes that didn't fit." The status quo was fulfilling, but my heart and God were guiding me towards my passion, and I could not ignore it. Years later, I now have my Ph.D. in Consumer, Apparel, and Retail Studies. My family and friends fondly refer to me as "Dr. Fashion." While my ultimate dream is to one day open my own apparel boutique, I am truly walking in my purpose everyday as a Fashion Merchandising professor in the "perfect pair of shoes." I am a professor and I impact the lives of fashion design and merchandising students because I "changed my shoes" and walked into God's destiny for me.

I desire my legacy to be one of giving. I try to live by the motto "You make a living by what you get, but you make a life by what you give." I hope I spend a lifetime giving love, encouragement, support, guidance, and sincerity to others.

Crystal's Track Shoes

By
Ms. Crystal Gay

Hello my name is Crystal Gay. I am the wife of Pastor Jerome Gay Jr., who is a loving and supportive husband. I am also a proud mother of two beautiful children, Jamari Gay (8) and Jordan Gay (2). As a stay-at-home mom and wife, I could not have asked for a better job. I am truly honored to be a servant for Christ and His people.

When my mother became pregnant with me, she was in college. Like any parent, you want the best for your child. Unfortunately, most of my family wanted her to have an abortion, so that she could finish school. But, praise be to God, she chose not to do it. It was a long journey for her, but through the years my purpose for being here became clear. As I look back now, I see how God used me in so many ways and that speaks volumes as to how much He loves me.

June of 1997 was a life changing moment for me, as I surrendered my life to Christ. He showed me how He saved me a second time. As I mentioned earlier, the first time, He saved me from not entering the world at all and the second time, He saved me from a life of sin.

In my lifetime I've experienced so much that has drawn me closer to the Lord. Some of those obstacles represented track shoes. I grew up as an only child, which was obstacle number one. It had its advantages because my mother made sure I did not grow up being selfish and inconsiderate of others. I had two male cousins that also played a role in that. I still to this day see them as my older brothers.

My parents got married after I was born. Therefore, to me, I had a normal life by having two parents. The tragedy is that my father was there, without actually being there. He lived with my mother and me, but was not emotionally or spiritually there to support us. Unfortunately, he got trapped in living a double lifestyle. He was a husband, father, brother, deacon in the church, and friend to many. However, his other life embraced the people in the streets, who were selling and using drugs. He also spent time around homosexuals. This would have not been an issue if God was the main priority in my father's life, but God was not.

As a young child I remember different experiences from which I knew only God saved us. There were times when my mother and I went grocery shopping at the store my father managed. One particular young boy would always follow us around. He was a bagboy at the grocery store.

There were many times when the phone rang throughout the night and early hours of the morning. I could hear my mom fussing and slamming down the phone. At that time, I did not fully understand what was going on. I was around eight or nine years old when I finally started putting together pieces of the puzzle. It came out that my father was cheating on my mother. He was stealing from church and his job, as well as hanging around drug dealers. My mother decided enough was enough. She knew she had to protect me.
Needless to say, this began to anger me and hatred set in. Seeing this made me start to doubt God. I questioned if He was real. I

knew what I was learning in church about God being wonderful, almighty, and all knowing, but I couldn't understand why He would allow such things to happen. As time went on, my hatred towards my father grew deeper. I lost all respect for him, even to the point of cursing at him. At this point in my life, I had a small group of people that I trusted, but the entire time I knew that God was still dependable. My mother would always take me riding, so that we could talk. The more she talked to me, the clearer the image of my hardened heart became to her.

One of the things that I've always respected and loved about my mom was that no matter how bad someone treated her, she demonstrated consistent forgiveness. It took me a while to catch on, especially since I wasn't saved. My mom's actions spoke louder than words. If she could help someone, she would, as long as it was legal. There were times that my father would come to her because he didn't have food or a job and she would help him. In my mind, this made absolutely no sense, as I thought he deserved to suffer. He was the one who turned his back on us. But, she showed me the love of Christ in how she loved my dad.

The prayers, talks, and examples from my mother continued. In August 1995, I became a freshman at, then-St. Augustine's College (now St. Augustine's University). I was excited to leave my world behind, but hated to leave my mother because I wasn't there to make sure she would be protected. I now see how God had to get me alone to develop everything my mother and family members instilled in me. I had to practice forgiveness in order to love as Christ did.

In June 1997, I was home for the summer break, working a fulltime job to help with my school expenses. I remember this day like it was yesterday. It was on a Sunday that I was scheduled to work, but I was the key holder for Afterthoughts, meaning I had to open the store. My mother and I went to church with the plan of leaving early to get me lunch before I went to work. I cannot tell you what the sermon title was for that day, nor do I remember what was preached. My mind was focused on time, as I couldn't be late for work.

The next thing I knew, people were praising God all over the church. I moved to the back, so that I was closer to the door. The funny thing is that I kept sending my little cousin over to get my mother's attention, but she showed me a look that said, "Don't rush the Spirit." I was not happy.

My raging attitude began to feel like water being thrown on fire. I began to cry, not knowing what I was crying for. My flesh felt confused and a bit crazy, but the Holy Spirit knew exactly what was going on. I remember hearing God say, "If you leave now without surrendering your life to me, your time will be up." God started bringing my past before me, showing how He protected me over and over again. He showed me how He loved me, even when I did not show that I loved Him. He sent messages through so many people and most of them were not saved. God was gracious enough to bring all of those things to my memory and the question was, "What are you waiting for?" I got saved that day and needless to say, I never did make it to work.

Later, I told my father that I forgave him. Once I did that, I felt like a free little bird that just learned how to fly. By learning to forgive, I was able to help others who were burdened in that area. If God hadn't forgiven us, where would we be? Ephesians 4:32 (KJV) says, "And be ye kind one to another, tenderhearted, forgiving one another, even as God for Christ's sake hath forgiven you."

With God allowing me to go through my life experiences, I never imagined, thought, or even dreamed I would have found my Adam, Mr. Jerome Gay Jr., at St. Augustine's College. This man has done a wonderful job of loving me, as Christ loved His bride, the church.

I hope to one day leave a legacy for my children and their children's children of forgiveness. I want them to know that forgiveness is of God. Without it, we can't be a part of Him. I truly thank God for using me to be an example of His love towards my family, friends, and community. I love to share my testimony so that people can see that I am only human—just like them. My husband always describes me as very patient and gentle. Others describe me as a realist, but in a godly way.

I used to feel like I had to be someone else after I got saved. However, God told me that He only created one Crystal Lashonda Best, who was from the small town of Wilson, NC. I had the job description that no one else could fulfill.

My vision is to continue to be an example to my children of a godly woman and wife. I expect that one day, my daughter will be a wife and my son will be a husband. I pray that they both find their soul mates, with God's guidance, so that they can continue to help and support our community.

I look at my life and I am honored that God chose me way before the beginning of time to be His humble servant. He chose me to share His word with those who don't know Him. He chose me to simply show love.

I can truly say that track shoes best represent my life. I was grounded while running my race. I jumped over many hurdles but the reward was reaching and crossing the finish line. As one of the old church songs says, "Victory is mine." I know that as long as God has me here on this earth, there will be races to run. I am confident that He will continue to strengthen me as I run and His Holy Spirit will enable me to finish each race in His time. So the track shoes must always be ready.

Jyia's Rock Climbing Shoes

By
Ms. Jyia Lindsey

My name is Jyia Angelic Haygood Lindsey. I am a follower of Christ striving to finish my purpose. I am a wife and a mother, who is learning everyday how important my role is. I am also a compassionate friend, who has learned through many failed relationships how to view others the way Christ views me. I am a lover of people because God created us. Last but not least, I am a dream merchant. I love to see and help others achieve their dreams. I enjoy taking time to encourage people, to counsel them, and to ensure that they know they are not alone in pursuing their dreams. I remind people that they were created with a purpose and that God has a plan for their lives.

I am blessed because I am chosen by God. He has allowed me to achieve the dream of becoming a wife and a mother. I am married to the man of my dreams and he has given me two children. I am grateful to have experienced birthing my own child. My son is my greatest accomplishment and I am so honored to be his mother. I am grateful for a marriage that has been ordained and kept by God and one that is ministering to people that God is more powerful than anything. I am grateful for having a successful blended family, where

138

we have worked together to ensure a happy environment for the kids involved. God has allowed me to defy the odds and demonstrate that through Him, children can have a stepparent who genuinely loves them. Women can see that we can work together to create a loving family dynamic for our children, no matter what. I am also grateful for having such a great support system in my friends and family.

Growing up and even now, I find myself to be a minority among my friends because I come from a two-parent home. Although I have always considered myself blessed to have had my father in my life, I have found that what I am most grateful for is the model of a godly marriage that my parents provided for me. I can proudly say that I learned how to be a wife, not from television, but from my mother. I watched and emulated her because she provided me with a beautiful example of what a wife, mother, and daughter of God looks like. And my father, the first man I ever loved, demonstrated how a husband should treat his wife and how a man leads his house, as he follows Christ. Through this union, I was provided with what I needed to achieve my dream of one day becoming a godly wife and mother.

As a child, I dreamed of many things, ranging from being an Olympic track athlete like Flo Jo; a teacher like my mother; a doctor and a wife/mother. However, as I grew and began to experience life, many of those dreams began to be better defined as hobbies or outside interests. I always strived to please my parents and being taught to respect my elders, I took that literally often to my own hurt.

Early in my life, I decided I wanted to be a doctor and I began working toward this goal in school, making sure I took the right classes, and got good grades. I even researched colleges and scholarships. After graduating from high school, I was accepted to a number of colleges to which I had applied. I knew my major would be Pre-Med, the necessary step to prepare for my journey to medical school. I was fortunate enough to have family members who attended and graduated college before me. Because of this, my parents felt the better choice would be to attend the same school. Although I had my own plans of where I wanted to study, when presented with the opportunity to win scholarships to attend the "family" school, I agreed to explore their summer program.

After excelling in the pre-freshman program given by NASA, I was enticed again with the idea of scholarships and being able to go to school for free. However, there was one condition: I had to change my major from Pre-Med to Engineering to qualify. So now, at eighteen years old, I must make a decision that could potentially set the course for the rest of my life. The similarities between my dream career and the scholarship opportunity both required an affinity for math and science, which happened to be my two favorite subjects. Since I was gifted in both of these areas I felt comfortable with what seemed to be a seamless transition. All I had to do was sign on the dotted line and the promise of a free college education would be mine. Well, you know how they say, "When something seems too good to be true, it is?" Well, they were right. After signing on the dotted line and changing my major, I embarked on my journey to obtain an Electrical and Computer Engineering degree.

As I began to get deeper into the core courses, it became painfully obvious that this was not what I wanted to do with my life. I encountered many challenges while "surviving and persevering" toward graduation. During this time, I was taught so many valuable lessons about life and about myself, but more importantly, I began to learn the purpose that God had for my life. I learned to never give up, and that sometimes dreams change. I still have a love for medicine and on some level I live with the regret of being so easily swayed from what I really wanted to do. Although I have been able to make a great life for myself through my engineering degree, I always wonder what my life would have been like had I become a doctor as planned. But before I ever get too far into what could have been, I'm able to look at my wonderful husband and my beautiful son and I'm sobered by the grace of God, in that He didn't give me what I thought I wanted.

My story most represents the rock climbing shoe. I have learned to continue to climb higher in my spiritual life, my purpose, my marriage, and my desire to be the best wife and mother I can be. Through my struggles and through God showing me how He could use the very thing I hated to mold me into what He wants me to be, I have found unspeakable joy. You see, through obtaining my engineering degree despite dropping out, failing my first class, and not becoming a doctor, I found God for myself. I had to learn how to depend on my faith and the support system He provided for me. With that, I continue on my journey to climb to higher heights and achieve things that I didn't know I would or could. That is not to say I don't get frustrated with what has happened or wonder what would have happened in my life.

Overall, God always gives me His peace and reminds me that it is not my will, but His will. Although I have come to find peace in my life and with my decisions, I vowed that I will always encourage those I meet, especially my husband, to follow your dreams until God gives you the command to follow another plan. It is vital to dream and to follow your dream so that you can live without regrets. Whenever I leave this world, hopefully no time soon, I want to leave knowing that I made a difference. When people hear my name, I want a smile or a fond thought to come to them. I want them to remember that life is a gift.

I want people to be able to say that I loved hard; that I was a protector and a supporter. I pray that those who know me will say that I sought to make a difference, one person at a time. Hopefully, my friends will be able to say that I always made time for them. I have tried to demonstrate my commitment to my family so that they will say that I never let the opportunity pass to show my love for them.

I want people to know that I loved God and family. I want them to know that I stood for righteousness. But most importantly, I want them to know that I lived my dream. Through my marriage, I pray that I can touch someone's life and be a living example of how God can transform a marriage into a godly model for others. I pray that through my son, I can offer him a reflection of Christ's unconditional love and a model of what a godly wife and mother looks like. I pray that each and every person with whom I have come into contact will be positively affected by my presence. I was not a big dreamer as a child because I was a logical thinker and I was honestly afraid to dream big. But what I am finding is that God gave me a mate, who does dream big and it's starting to rub off on me. He's made me feel safe in dreaming big because in doing so, I must realize I cannot rely on my own ability. I must depend on God's infinite power.

My participation in this project reflects my sincerest desire to touch a girl or woman, who believes she has to live out someone else's dream. I want her to learn from my mistake. I hope she will know that she cannot please everyone. She must refuse to give up on her dream. Lastly, I hope that my story will breathe life into a woman who may feel that it's too late to pursue her dreams.

Jo's Saddle Shoes, Combat Boots, High Heels, and Flats

By
Dr. Josephine Hamilton

Greetings in the name of the Lord! My name is Josephine Alexander Hamilton. I answer to many other names: Jo, Poogie, JoJo, Mom, Nana, "Bunky," or Dr. Jo. My life-walk has taken me from saddle shoes to combat boots to gorgeous high heels (and flats sometime). My self-description is really a puzzle of many precious parts created by the strong women in my life. No one part is really bigger or broader than another but all represent the "bits-and-pieces" that form my very being.

I am:

- a daughter, granddaughter, and great-granddaughter;
- a sister and friend;
- a military veteran and military (retired) spouse;
- a wife, mother, and "Nana;" and
- an educator.

Although my family has been and is blessed with the strong presence of male leadership, there is an equally dominant presence of strong, focused, and tenacious women who have shaped my life. My blessings are these women and the lessons they have given and continue to give me.

I attribute my genes to Mariah Alexander and Nannie Hudson, my fraternal and maternal grandmothers. These women never let their souls or soles wear thin. They cloaked themselves in the armor of God that empowered them to be helpmates to husbands and givers of love to large families and extended families. Unfortunately, I never met Miss Mariah (Mama); but the endless affectionate stories about her strength and unyielding belief in God have always had an invisible steadying hand on my shoulders. I am told that Miss Hudson referred to me as "the Lady" at the moment of my birth. Truly blessed, I had her in my life for twenty three years. Miss Hudson had quiet moxie! Whether astounded or outraged by situations, her response was always a compelling, "Do Jesus!"

In an era when older black women were referred to as Auntie, she would boldly tell white nickel-insurance and door salesmen, "We are not related, so do not call me Auntie." On more than one occasion in the darkness of night, she hid or walked one of her children to the outskirts of town to safety. She nursed my mother to recovery from burns and asthma attacks. And, no matter the elected purpose, Ms. Hudson would carefully pin her hat, firmly grasp her pocketbook, and walk to the polls to place her vote.

My grandmothers, Katherine Alexander and Eunice Beatrice Harris lived generations ahead of their times. Katherine (fraternal grandmother), as a single parent, understood the importance of maintaining connections to the family-core. While meeting the challenges of being a single parent, she reared her children using the collective wisdom of her family. Eunice (known as Monday) was the quintessential renaissance woman. Never afraid of challenges, she once out-ran a Model T. Her strong constitution allowed her to bury three husbands. Monday was a woman of determination. She was resolute in her decision to give her child the best in life, to be the best cook, and to stand up firmly for her rights! She managed to pull her family from the brink of devastation, providing financial sustenance. She regretted being unable to raise her own child while she served as a surrogate mother to other people's children. Monday never begged or groveled. Instead, she leaned on the everlasting arms of God and made it through. Both of my grandmothers tightly knitted together their families and never let the soles of their shoes rest in one place for too long.

My mother, Doris Lee Reese Alexander, devoted and still devotes her life to her children. Although she never sat in a college or university classroom, she emphasized the importance of education and taught me to never give up. Case in point: although our family was Methodist, my Mom dressed me at age six and took me to enroll in a prominent Catholic school. After a long visit with the principal, I was denied entry because of the color of my skin. My mother took me by the hand and told me to walk out of that office with my head held high. At that young age I was taught to look medical providers directly in their eyes and tell them my issues. I was taught to speak clearly, listen closely, and answer appropriately. My mother instilled in me how "ladies" should conduct themselves and how an impeccable appearance speaks volumes. She explained the importance of being proud but not to the point of dishonoring God's word. When a Home Economics teacher told my mother that I did not have the aptitude for sewing—although she could not sew—my mother picked me up early from school, took me to purchase a sewing machine, lining, and fabric so that I could make a winter coat. My teacher was astounded! The lesson: never be defined by others.

My Mom imparted the idea that shyness may be limiting but demureness is powerful. She advocated treating everyone with respect but reacting appropriately when disrespected. According to my Mom, "Jesus wasn't afraid to love, so why should you be afraid to love." Her foundations for success are having a firm belief in God; being a rock-solid helpmate; building a solid family; and having self-assurance. This woman was and is the soul anchor of her family and made sure everyone's souls were spiritually fed and that their soles never wore thin.

These women, their traits, and the lessons I have obtained are what have led me to make important choices in my life. I began an early career in public speaking, civic engagement, and service. After college, I boldly marched into the military recruiting office and asked for the people that gave direct commissions. I listened patiently (maybe even demurely) as an Army Sergeant explained why I needed to enlist "to learn the Army from the bottom-up" and not start as a commissioned officer. I remember shaking his hand firmly, thanking him and asking, "Who do I talk to about being commissioned?" In three months' time, I received commission as a Second Lieutenant in the Army.

Because I know that God knows best and as the old saying goes "God takes care of fools and babies," I was not afraid to love. I got engaged within two-weeks of meeting a man, and married him four months later. Fast forward thirty five years later—that love is still strong! My belief in the Almighty and God-given self-assurance helped me to navigate the challenges of relocating my family every time my husband was given a new assignment. Each move meant finding another job. Daily prayer and meditation strengthened me to accept positions that I would normally reject. I taught English as a Second Language (when I had not known it was even a course of study), edited a bi-weekly military newspaper, and managed a staff that did not speak English. I did not allow my pride to keep me from accepting positions that appeared to be lesser than my qualifications and experience. I leaned on the everlasting arms of God and made it through.

My reasons for pursuing a Doctoral degree were less than grand. I simply wanted to prove to myself that I could do it. It took all the genetic fiber, silent prayers, invisible hugs and kisses from the women in my life to reach my goal. What began as a personal test has morphed into a better understanding of what God really wanted me to do. Even now, God has not finished building me. Because of my love of education, communication, and helping others, He has led me to work with people who are heartbroken and bereaved.

God gave me the strength to build a solid family. He blessed me to be a wife and mother of two sons. Watching them grow into men of honor is an even greater blessing. My good fortune continues as I watch my eldest son and his wife build a solid family with my four grandchildren. I have the honor of doing things with my grandchildren that I did not have time to do as a parent. My blessings include: listening to elementary and preschool jokes that really do not connect; kissing away tears; giving long baths; and most of all listening to future dreams.

What would I like my legacy to be?

- That I honor God;
- That I loved and *am* loved;
- That I gave my best and held back nothing;
- That my past was necessary to provide for my future;
- That the sound and remembrance of my name and likeness bring sweet memories and not bitter reflections;
- That I loved and *was* loved;
- That my family endures, endures, and endures;
- That my family honors God;
- **That I Honored God**.

"Do Jesus!"

Tamika's Stilettos and Tennis Shoes

By
Ms. Tamika Lynn

My name is Tamika Lynn. Most people with whom I have frequent contact would consider me to be direct, confident, and a perfectionist. However, the real "me" is meshed somewhere in between. If I were to describe myself, I would say that I am self-conscious, goal oriented, prideful, and driven. As much as I would love to always be that confident person that everyone sees, I am certainly a work in progress. Opening up and sharing who I really am with others can be frightening because it forces me to really examine myself.

My self-consciousness goes way back. Well, maybe not that far. I am only in my thirties. At times, being self-conscious can be a good thing, but in my case there is nothing good about my self-consciousness. The precursor to my self-consciousness perhaps began while I was in elementary school. I was born in another country and migrated to the United States at a fairly young age. When I began school, my teachers were concerned about my understanding of the English language. Though I thought my English was perfect, my teachers and classmates begged to differ. I was offered extra help to catch up and accepted the assistance. I thought my classmates would accept me because I was trying hard to bridge the language barrier. But of course they found even more things to tease me about, from my last name, to where I was born, to my clothes, tennis shoes, and even my socks. I was subject to ridicule on a daily basis. There was no right with these kids.

I know you are probably saying, "All kids get teased;" just find new friends. Well, when you have moved to a new country and attend school five days a week, your pool of friends typically come from your school. No matter what I did and how much progress I made, I began to feel like I was never good enough. That feeling of not being good enough is like a record in my head that someone placed on repeat. Therefore, I give 100 percent hoping that I am deemed as good enough, but the crazy thing is, even when I give 100 percent, I often doubt myself. I have received awards in both my career and athletics. I have also gotten promotions. But, I always hear a voice saying, "You could have done better."

I am certainly still a work in progress and through my six year old daughter, yes a six year old, I am slowly coming to grips with the fact that I am good enough. When I speak positivity into my daughter's life, she blesses me with her positive words of affirmation. Yes, it took a six year old to break that cycle of me thinking that I was not good enough. Who needs a therapist when I have my daughter? It took more than 30 years to break the cycle, but as Steve Harvey says, "Don't trip, He ain't through with me yet." My experience as a youth was certainly a tennis shoes without the sparkles moment. It can only get better.

Now that I have shared with you, I would like to take you on an abbreviated journey. I mentioned earlier that I was goal oriented. I know that people say everyone should set goals, but I honestly do not remember when I became obsessed about setting goals. I remember learning that you should write down your goals because when you see them, they are no longer thoughts. They become more tangible—to the point that they come alive where you can breathe, see, smell, and taste them.

I first began setting goals because my mom always encouraged me to achieve more than she did. Therefore, I practically wrote everything down. Writing down small things seemed to work for me. When I recorded my goals, I pushed myself to achieve them. It did not matter whether it meant doing a few more math problems, watching a little less television, or reading extra pages in a book. I did it and discovered success. I did not want to become that person in my old neighborhood who would say, "I've always wanted to . . ." So, I stuck with a method that worked for me.

After living in Florida, I wanted to live somewhere different. But, this time it was on my own terms. I set goals that would prepare me for the next chapter of my life, which was college. I ran my way out of Florida (literally). You see, I ran Track and Field and was offered several athletic scholarships. I had accomplished my goal. Thus, allowing me to leave Florida on my terms. The funny thing about setting goals is that you may not complete them on your timeline. My former pastor used to say, "Pray until something happens (PUSH)." For example, I wanted to attend graduate school immediately after I completed my undergraduate studies, but that goal did not go according to my plan. I went back to school some ten years later and believe I was more prepared because of life experiences. I followed the path God had for me, on His time. I am a firm believer that it is never too late!

If everything was easy and happened on our terms, then everyone would be successful. I had to be diligent to accomplish the things that I set out to do. Yes, I was discouraged when I did not meet a goal on my terms, but I amended my timelines and kept on moving.

I realized that when I put my mind to something and paired it with hard work and diligent hands, my days of wearing sneakers would be over, even if I did graduate to the sneakers with sparkles. My shoes of choice are now high heel pumps in basic colors black, brown, and taupe.

Now, let's move on to something that drives some people crazy, but has worked in my favor. What I deem as having pride, others consider being a perfectionist with a mild case of Obsessive Compulsive Disorder (OCD). I told you I was meshed somewhere in between. Having pride in what you do and giving your all to a task will always be received favorably. Having pride and setting goals has gotten me an athletic scholarship, a 3.5 grade point average (GPA) in my undergraduate studies, a 3.9 (GPA) in my graduate studies, a career that I love, with promotions that I never expected.

My mother instilled a sense of pride in me. She gives 100 percent to everything she does. She says, "When your name is attached to something, you should always put your best foot forward." When my mom was younger, she always had what we call a 'side hustle.' I can remember my mom cleaning my friend's house. She never cut corners. My mom cleaned that house, as she did our own—on her hands and knees. My mom drilled in me the practice of taking pride in my work. This is something I try to instill in my daughter, as well as the people I manage. My daughter has taken this pride thing to a whole new level. She says to my husband and me, "I don't just want to be a good daughter; I want to be a great daughter." I believe she heard the expression from a movie and changed the words around to suit her needs. If I have instilled pride in my daughter, we are going to have a bright future.

Driven is what I am. Everything that I have experienced proves that my approach works. My self-consciousness, goal setting (like a mad woman) habits and immense pride motivate me to go to the next level. As long as God is blessing me and doors are opening, why not? I believe God wants everyone to use their talents and to be diligent. That is what I do and will continue to do.

Those children back in elementary school, contributed to who I am today. Surely we would not have migrated to a land of opportunity if there were no opportunities. I have found that there are tons of prospects, if you believe and apply yourself.

I am driven because I want to set a good example for my family, my daughter, and anyone that is on the outside looking in. I am hoping to lead my daughter and others by example. You will notice that most of what I have shared with you all ties together. I did not plan for it to be this way and felt very scattered at first. I mentioned that examining and sharing who I am was frightening, but I feel as though sharing with you has helped me to grow. I typically reflect on my birthday, like most do, but my reflecting was more like a beat up session and no more. As I write everything down that I have achieved, I now realize that my life is not bad at all. I am doing what I am supposed to be doing in God's time, not mine.

The Lord has truly ordered my steps. As I write, I hear a song in my head that is one of my favorites. One of the lines says, "Order my steps in your word dear Lord, lead me guide me every day." I am truly thankful for everything I have achieved and for everything I will achieve. I am not proud that I thought someone (me) God created was not good enough. But, I am thankful that my daughter looks at me and tells me all the reasons why I am good enough. She does not even understand that she is blessing me. But, she does it with a pure heart.

I would like to be remembered as a kind person, with a bubbly personality. I would like to be known for giving 100 percent to all that I did, without having to be in the spotlight. My family and friends will remember me for always trying to set good examples, always encouraging them to do their best, and always willing to give my last.

I want the people I know to believe that the world is a better place because I was fortunate enough to pass through it in a particular season. I want them to remember that during my season of life that I displayed a generous amount of love and kindness without expecting anything in return.

Remember, I am still growing. I am still a work in progress and God is certainly not through with me yet. As I continue to grow and walk with God on my journey, I am now wearing my shoes of choice—stilettos.

Cassie's Civil Servant
and Cooking Shoes

By
Ms. Cassandra Bumbry

My name is Cassandra (Cassie) Bumbry. I am a woman committed to growing closer to God and one who strives on a daily basis to increase my faithfulness and obedience through education, prayer, and self-reflections. God blessed me with two wonderful adult children and eight awesome grandchildren. I am passionate about cooking and one of my greatest joys is watching family and friends enjoy my labor of love. Last but not least, I am a dedicated federal government reemployed annuitant budget director with God-given analytical abilities and people skills.

Although I have always considered myself "spiritual," my formal relationship with God was spotty for a number of years. In the last fifteen years or so, I have been a God loving, faithful, and consistent church member. Although my parents were "brought up in the church" church attendance was almost nonexistent. A neighbor who decided to teach bible study to the neighborhood kids during the summer was responsible for making me aware of God. As a teen I occasionally went to church with my best friend and throughout most of my adulthood, I attended church intermittently. I must say that although my church attendance was hit or miss, I have always been aware of God.

It's amazing what you retain without realizing it. The information provided during the summer months in the neighborhood bible school stayed with me and sustained me through some rough patches in my childhood. From my early teen years to the present, God's presence was always felt. God has sustained me through many trials and tribulations, from the mundane to the miraculous, through sickness and health as well as happy or sad times. I owe this awesome and unbelievable life I've lived to God and I give Him all the glory.

When I look back over my life, the good, the bad and the crazy all merge together to create the person I've become. What I know for sure is that God, in all of His wisdom and mercy, knows your heart. From the sickly child I was to the active senior I am today, God has shown me favor. There have been so many blessings in my life, starting with my children and grandchildren. I had a troubled childhood, but that was a blessing because it helped to form the person that I have become.

Throughout my life there have always been angels there for me in the form of teachers, neighbors, managers, and friends. These people saw more potential in me than I could ever imagine. From the neighborhood grocery store owner who picked me, out of all the children in the neighborhood, to work for her, to all the managers who always had confidence in me to get the job done. Only God knew how much fear I felt.

My childhood years were rough, especially once my parents separated. My mom was a single woman raising four kids, with little support from my dad. My maternal grandmother lived with us intermittently and tried to help out. The burden of it all became overwhelming for my mother and alcohol abuse became an issue for us. I say us because alcohol abuse affects everyone in the household.

During those years, I was given a lot of responsibility as it relates to caring for my brothers and the household. Junior and senior high school were particularly difficult for me. Not because I got in trouble, but because I was so introverted I wanted to blend in with the wall. At home, we never knew when my mother would be drinking and become physically and mentally abusive. No one ever inquired about school work or home work. I showed up at school every day, usually ate lunch in the empty classroom and tried not to bring any attention to myself or the situation at home.

I decided that I would forgo the regular high school to attend a vocational high school. The main reason was that I knew college was probably not going to be an option. This way, I would have a skill that would allow me to get a decent job after graduation. In a vocational high school, you have the regular academic classes, e.g., math, English, geography, etc., but you also had four classes a day that concentrated on a trade. In my case, my trade concentration was business. It included typing, shorthand, business machines, and business English.

I need to take a detour to talk about other significant things that impacted my life, particularly my senior year. You see I gave birth to a son the summer before my senior year. My school never knew I was pregnant and my mother did not know, until I was eight months along. The circumstances of the pregnancy are for another book or story. Suffice to say, that summer was very eventful. I gave birth on July 7, 1965 and nearly died from a ruptured appendix a week later. God had His work cut out for Him during this period in my life. Although I had very little prenatal care, I gave birth to a healthy son. On the other hand, in the two weeks after his birth, I suffered with migraines; was diagnosed with severe anemia; and had a ruptured appendix. I was hospitalized for most of July. I recuperated in August and was back in school and working in September. God's hands were all over my life.

My senior year, I started working for the government, first as a clerk-trainee for the DC Government and later as a permanent clerk-stenographer in a typing pool for the Department of Treasury. By the time we were seniors, all of my business classmates had passed the civil service test and were eligible to get permanent jobs with the government. Out of some thirty or so classmates, I was the only one sent to the Department of Treasury, Office of the Secretary while all the others were sent to the Department of Transportation, Federal Aviation Administration. I was very upset and could not imagine why my teacher would do such a thing to me. I now know that it was divine intervention and God's hand was again all over my life.

Although I graduated and passed the Office of Personnel Management typing test, I have to admit I was a horrible typist. After three months of typing terror God sent me on a detail to the accounting office, where my typing speed and accuracy were not required. The detail turned into a permanent job and it was the beginning of my incredible career.

In the beginning, the word "career" was not how I characterized what I had. I worked! As a matter of fact the word "goal" was not part of my vocabulary either. I worked! I was a scared young lady, with responsibilities and a mouth to feed, who could not or would not fail. I always had a strong work ethic and worked hard at whatever I did. I realized I had a career when I allowed myself to feel confident about my God-given skills and abilities and the impact my position had on others.

God has guided my career path from my initial interview as a high school senior with the Department of Treasury until my re-employment after retirement. Throughout my career, which has spanned almost forty five years, I've only had two job interviews and beyond that I never once had to seek a job. I've held positions in finance and human resources and I loved every position and managed to always find the fun in them.

Over the course of my career, many people gave me advice or opportunities that helped accelerate my career. I believe that all of them were put in my path by God. You see, I did not have minor things happening to me. They were all major. The promotions I never asked for; the awards every year; so many "firsts" that I cannot remember them all. One thing that was a constant and still is in my career is the relationship with my peers and managers. I was usually the only person of color in the room. This meant there were no footprints for me to follow. God always stepped in and never once allowed me to feel intimidated by anyone.

I've enjoyed an outstanding life and career. It seemed that opportunities abounded for me. I retired as a GS-15 Finance Director, but I was blessed to have had other opportunities that included: Secretary-Treasurer for the Treasury Department Welfare Association; Treasury Department Federal Credit Union Volunteer Loan Officer; Treasury Department Federal Credit Union Board Member; Member of IRS Chief Counsel EEO Advisory Board; and I was accepted to the Georgetown Executive Development Program.

If I had to sum up what the key to my success is—it's really very simple. Be curious! I am curious about everything. This curiosity was the key to everything! My manager, co-workers and people outside my organization knew that I knew a little something about everything and if I could not answer their questions, I could point them in the right direction. When a question was asked of me, I've never once said, "That's not my job." My advice to you . . . Don't limit yourself.

I hope that after I am gone, people will say I was kind, fair, compassionate, funny, and loved the Lord. Of course, they will talk about my cooking! I have always strived to be a "good person" and I think for the most part I am. We all have our demons and I am certainly not exempt from that. I want my children and grandchildren to know without question that I love them. I want my mom to know that I forgive her and love her very much. I hope that I continue to make a difference in the lives of my family and friends.

I want young people to understand that no matter what obstacles appear in your path, they need to take them to God and trust Him to work things out. There have been so many terrible things that have happened in my life and I thought the situations were hopeless. But God fixed them. Also, understand that everyone will go through valleys at some point in life. Just remember, it is all for the good. Every trial has a good purpose, at least all of mine did. Take time to be still and hear God. Hitting the pause button every now and then is therapeutic. I hope that my story will inspire girls and women to never give up on themselves, because God never gives up on us.

Claudette's Hiking Boots

By
Ms. Claudette Davis

And ye shall seek me, and find me, when ye shall search for me with all your heart. And I will be found of you, saith the LORD; and I will turn away your captivity, and I will gather you from all the nations, and from all the places whither I have driven you, saith the Lord; and I will bring you again into the place whence I caused you to be carried away captive. Jeremiah 29:13-14 (KJV)

"Finding God in our Everyday Life" is the title of the book my spiritual brother/friend, Jack, teasingly encouraged me to use, as I shared how I continue to have these strange and yet wonderful encounters with God. An example of this occurred one day as I drove to work, stressing over the challenges I was going to face. As I pulled into the parking lot, ready to turn off the car, the radio played "I'm At Peace" by Vicki Yohe. That was just enough to get me through the day. On another occasion, God pressed me to put gas in the tank of a friend's car (on a credit card that was maxed out except for $47). When I arrived home, there was a refund check from an over paid bill in the amount of $47 on the counter; a check from the gas company of all things. Still another time was when I was preparing for a difficult situation, by reading Psalm 18:2 (KJV)

"The Lord is my Rock . . ." When I stepped out of my car onto the black top parking lot, there laid a rock the size of a strawberry. No other rock like this was in sight. It was as if God was saying, "I don't want you to forget what you just read about Me when you go into that situation." Yeah, in these situations it wasn't so hard to "find" God and see His handy work in my life. A positive-minded person can trace Him in the blessings. But, what about when we are in the storms!

I've heard it said that "When you can't trace God you can trust Him." Every time I would hear this statement, I would become uneasy, as it just didn't sit well in my spirit. I knew that in Hebrews 13:5 (KJV), God said, " . . . I will never leave thee, nor forsake thee" so how it could be true that you couldn't trace Him? Well in 2012, God showed me why this was not true in my life through the death of my four-year-old niece and six months later, my two-year-old cousin. Both girls' deaths were sudden and tragic. All the words of comfort could not make sense of this. I mean, we were still reeling from the death of my 3-month-old nephew, who passed away just 18 months prior from Sudden Infant Death Syndrome. Time and time again, I would hear "when you can't trace Him . . ." even during the services! I had to lean hard on God and dig deep into His Word for the words to share with my loved ones and the parents of these three babies. My Babies! I felt so challenged to put this lie to rest.

Sometimes it takes these types of circumstances to make God's Word as real as our breath and apply them to our lives. As I recorded these events, re-read previous entries and searched the bible for understanding and comfort, Jeremiah 29:13 jumped off the page. Ah, ha! I could see that I needed to put on my hiking Boots if I was going to find God in all this hurt, pain, and confusion. God wanted to be found and I would have to be intentional in my search for Him. Boy, did I find Him.

I found God in the many calls from friends who didn't know the parents, but knew me. They knew I would need them to carry me, as I carried my family. I found God as I cried on my pillow and heard in the background songs playing on the radio that were so appropriate for the questions running through my mind. I found God when I reflected on the summer trip to Haymarket, VA, where I enjoyed the fellowship of two of my girlfriends whose "off da chain" hospitality, laughter, food, and fun lifted my spirits. We dangled our feet in the community pool, relaxed and basked in God's love and our love for each other. Yes, I saw that God had prepared and strengthened me for the news of the pool accident that claimed my niece's life one week later. I could find God (as I looked back) the morning of December 24th when my pastor spoke about Mary, Jesus' mother, saying to the angel, "Be it unto me" when told she would carry the Christ Child. The radio played "Let the Church Say Amen" by Marvin Winans, as I traveled both to and from work that day. I thought it strange, until I entered my house to hear the sad news of my cousin dying in a car accident. Yes, after the shock, I realized I could "trace" God even in the midst of all this.

Like Peter, when we take our eyes off the Master, our situations and circumstances will lie to us and say we can't trace God. Don't listen to the lies; listen to the Truth. Hebrews 11:6 (KJV) promises us that "He is a rewarder of them that diligently seek him" and Deuteronomy 4:29 (KJV) tells us that "But if from thence thou shalt seek the Lord thy God, thou shalt find him, if thou seek him with all thy heart and with all thy soul." Yes, in the mess of life, the rocky places, the dry desert areas, and the unstable terrains, those cute red bottom pumps won't do. You're going to need sturdy heavy-duty, protective Hiking Boots so that you can dig real deep through all the 'stuff' to find God. Take it from me . . . He is There. I promise!

Rose's Nursing Shoes, Pumps, Penny Loafers, and Shoes with Spikes

By
Rosalie C. Randall

My name is Rosalie Chisolm Randall, a wife, mother, grandmother, and great grandmother, who has a strong belief in a Christian life. I am a part of the traditionalist generation and am now retired from the federal government in the field of nursing. I also served in the U.S. Army Reserve Nurse Corp for nearly twelve years. I trust God in everything I do and He is first and foremost in my decisions and situations. In my Christian life, I serve in my church through the health unit ministry and I sing in two choirs. First and foremost, I am blessed to have a supportive spouse who stands with me unconditionally. We discuss our issues and try to come up with a joint, suitable solution, no matter what we encounter. I am very thankful to have health, strength and the capacity to reach out to others and provide a compassionate and caring spirit, especially to those who are less fortunate.

I am happy to be the mother of six sons. Three of my sons are biological and two are blended through my second marriage.

However, through God's infinite wisdom, I fully embrace and love all of the boys as my children. In addition, a very dear friend to one of the boys came to live with us for a period of time; therefore, we adopted him into our hearts as our son. This addition to the family increased our number to six sons. I have a passion for helping others in need. For you see, my story includes the fact that I was adopted when I was thirteen days old. My adopted parents loved and provided for me throughout my adolescent and early adulthood, for which I am thankful. Therefore, I have an intense passion to give back to society by helping others because somebody cared for me. I know that I am blessed and highly favored by God.

I remember growing up as an only child, playing with my tea set and dolls, wearing my mother's high heel shoes. I spent a lot of time at home with my grandmother during the day because my other family members worked outside of the home. I would observe her as she diligently went through her daily chores: cooking, laundering, and cleaning house. This was a very good reflection of the strong shoes she filled in her love for us. At some point during my adolescence, my grandmother was diagnosed with diabetes. During that time she was often sick and eventually began to suffer with her legs and feet. I would often read scriptures from the bible to her and would rub and massage her legs to try to comfort her. Even though she was ill and was sometimes required to stay in bed, she taught me how to cook a pot of grits from her sick bed. Therefore, from a child I felt the need to take care of my grandmother, which was the beginning of my interest in being a care giver. My grandmother did not receive a formal education, but she had a PhD in wisdom and common sense. She was a caring person, who gave to others from the bottom of her heart and soul. There were many days that she shared her food with neighbors, who were less fortunate.

My kindergarten and first grade teacher wore good quality shoes and significantly impacted my life by exemplifying a loving, caring and gentle spirit. I loved her and always wanted to be like her, so much so, that I often would go home with her after school, with my parents' permission. We lived in the same neighborhood, so I would occasionally eat dinner at her home. I also often played the role of the teacher with my dolls or with my friends. My teacher was my idol during my pre-adolescent years and I was convinced that I would be a teacher, just like her. She left an indelible impression on me. As a result, I joined the Future Teachers of America club during my high school years. I enjoyed reading poems by Robert Frost and books that my mother read at her school.

There was a house with a little store in front in our neighborhood. That house was across from the elementary school, which sold candies, cookies and snowball icy cones. I remember there were several flavors to choose from. This was one of several stores in the community owned and managed by a woman in the neighborhood who had several children in her care. I don't ever remember seeing a father in the home or store. The store owner was always there and all of the children in the neighborhood respected her. Looking back on this leads me to see that she had a strong presence (strong and stable shoes) in the neighborhood, as an entrepreneur. I remember her as a kind-hearted soul.

My grandmother often sold peanuts and sodas whenever there was a baseball game in the park across the street from our home. She possessed strong salesmanship that reached deep into the souls of those persons purchasing her goods. I also made icy cups called "chilly bears" and sold them to neighboring children. Again, the strong souls of my family and neighbors were evident. It must be noted that all of this took place during the late 1940's and early 1950's. The women in my life wore well-built shoes, which laid the foundation for me in developing a good work ethic and learning how to make an honest dollar.

I attended elementary school and was fortunate to maintain good grades. I participated in many school activities, such as Girl Scouts. Becoming a scout and being an active member of the troop was a big thing for me, especially because I was the only child in the family and this made my family very proud of me. I learned some very important principles of life, such as discipline, organization, leadership, and socialization. I remember the uniform we wore quite well. It was green and buttoned down the front. Intermediate girls wore long sleeves with a Green Beret and yellow scarf. Wearing buster brown shoes and the scout uniform gave me a sense of belonging. The Girl Scouts impacted my life by strengthening self-confidence, courage, and character. It also taught me how to maintain physical and mental alertness, to be a good citizen, and to care for others. I remember saying the Girl Scout promise at our meetings while holding up the three middle fingers. I believe the soles of those buster brown shoes gave me courage and confidence to journey destiny's path. The unconditional love of my parents and being a Girl Scout taught me how to keep my feet in good shoes and establish a strong foundation in life.

As a teenager, my girlfriend and I wore our pumps to church on Sundays. After the service, we walked across town to visit our sick church members who were in local hospitals. Of course, the pumps made us feel grown up. We did not have any relatives or friends there but we would visit each patient, greet them, and wish them a speedy recovery. It was a big deal for us, especially when we saw a smile on their faces in return. I did not realize it at that time but we were doing God's work by making people feel better—by showing them that we cared. Those special pumps helped lay the foundation for my career in the nursing field.

My girlfriend and I walked to school daily, wearing penny loafers. However, many students had holes in the soles of their shoes, as they were worn over wet and icy ground. We learned to place a thin layer of cardboard or newspaper in our shoes to keep our feet warm and protected from the cold. This routine did not bother us because most of my school mates were in the same financial situation. However, some of us were fortunate to get our shoes repaired with a half sole or heel replacement. Based on the challenges and struggles that our forefathers went through wearing worn shoes or no shoes at all, this struggle gave me the strength and motivation to tread on to accomplish my goals and aspirations.

On another occasion, one of my homeroom teachers was sick and recuperating at home after surgery. I took the initiative and asked two of my classmates to join me to visit our teacher. When we arrived to her home, we cleaned, put out the trash, and comforted her during our visit. This effort really made our teacher feel better and lifted her spirits because she had students who cared. Again, this initiative was another reflection of wearing the shoes of a care giver, demonstrating "soul to sole," as a teenager.

At another point in my adolescent life, I remember working for a family that had a set of nine—month-old twins—a boy and a girl. It paid minimum wages for working all day, which was not a lot of money during those days. However, I was determined to work and make my own money. This was the beginning of my effort to earn my financial freedom. It gave me the opportunity to learn how to care for children.

As a small child, I didn't like many people fussing with my hair. My Aunt Lucille (the woman featured in the front section of this book) was the only person I felt comfortable enough with to comb and style my locks. I believe that that experience enticed me to try my hand at hair care and to take a high school class in cosmetology. It also was beneficial for me to learn how to style my own hair. In addition, the experience afforded me the opportunity to learn a great skill and to style the hair of my friends and neighbors. Learning cosmetology was another step taken to develop my business and entrepreneurial skills.

I had another job working at a restaurant as a bus girl. However, I probably weighed about 85 pounds that summer. The problem was that I could not pick up the tray to carry the dishes. It was too heavy. The owner and manager had compassion on me and reassigned me to work in the kitchen. When school opened again, my work hours interfered with my studies and I had to quit the job. However, based on my good work record, the owner arranged for me to babysit his children for a few hours a day while his wife managed payroll and other financial matters at the restaurant. I not only earned extra money while in school, but also maintained an account at one of the local savings bank. Putting away money for a rainy day was a lesson taught in my household and I am very thankful for that. This is another example of the strong shoes worn and the solid foundation built in my family.

Another life experience that I endured while in high school was giving birth to my first son. During this period, the stigma of having a child as a teenager was not acceptable and society looked down on you. However, my son was born with abundant love and affection from both maternal and paternal families. Through the grace of God I put on track shoes with spikes to persevere against the odds. I went back to high school and completed my education. Even though I was viewed negatively, I held my head high and graduated from high school.

My mother fully supported me through this endeavor. Even though she was a single parent, she wore real strong shoes with thick soles. She was determined to see that I received a good education and established a respectable and secure life. In my senior year of high school one of my teachers noticed my potential and encouraged me to go into nursing. I imagine she recognized my natural caregiving compassion that was demonstrated in my class work and in my concern for others. Therefore, she recommended that I attend nursing school. Another point I want to mention is that I used to play the part or pretend to be a nurse or doctor as a child. As you can see, the caregiving tendencies were apparent, but I could not visualize how my career path would develop. I finally accepted my calling to be a nurse and began to focus on this career choice. I was initially interested in going to an out-of-state college but was unable to fulfill this dream due to lack of finances.

In the meantime, I looked for a job in the local area. However, jobs were limited, even with a high school education. As a result, I went to an employment agency that placed people in jobs in northern states. All the while, I continued to focus on my goal, which was to complete college and obtain a nursing degree.

I left the local area for a job in a northern state with the support and blessings of my mother. Once on the job, I grew afraid because it was my first time away from home. Through the grace of God, one of my schoolmates arrived on the job the next day and we worked together, supporting one another. Eventually, we encountered some difficult challenges that prompted us to look for better paying jobs. We decided to relocate to a larger northern city where we had family and friends to support us. We met on a daily basis and traveled together, learning the big city while looking for work. Eventually we found work, again working together for the same company. We continued our employment together until the job had a reduction in employment. At that point, I went to the employment office and took a placement examination to qualify for a position at a major city hospital. I passed the examination a few weeks before my current job ended. Within two weeks of the layoff I started my first day of training to work at the new job and successfully completed the requirements.

It was unknown to me at the time, but I believe that God planned my career this way to see if I really believed that nursing was my calling. I was always thin and small in stature. To work with sick people you are required to be healthy and strong. Several of the senior nurses advised me to continue my education and to maintain a healthy life style. Later, the hospital offered employees the opportunity to train "free of charge" as a licensed practical nurse (LPN). The only stipulation was that the employee would commit to work at that hospital after the training was completed. However, I did not qualify for the program because I did not have seniority. I continued to work at the hospital and learned the basic skills of assisting and caring for patients.

In the meantime, there was time for fun with my family and friends. I remember the times that my colleagues, friends, and I would go shopping. We would purchase dresses and high heel shoes just alike. Yes, I have always been an avid shoe lover. I strongly believe one has to have a good foundation to succeed in life and the security of a good quality shoe with a strong sole motivates the soul. We would often go to dinner or to a theater to relax after a day of shopping. What a great way to unwind after the stressful week of work. We also took in the movies or visited museums and local parks. I frequently attended mass but was not deeply spiritual during this phase of my life. However, God continued to guide my footsteps. He led me down the right path to success.

The opportunity rolled around again for interested employees to sign up for the LPN training. At this point, I realized that no one in my department expressed an interest, so I placed my name on the list. Again, I was rejected due to seniority. Since I was determined to be a nurse, I called the school and found out all of the requirements and proceeded to take the entrance examination. I studied hard and kept it quiet because I did not want anyone to deter or discourage me. I successfully passed the examination and interviewed with the director of the school who wore strong shoes. I shared with her my attempts to enroll in the training and the denials based on my low seniority at the hospital. However, it all worked out and I was allowed to attend the LPN training. I successfully graduated. I subsequently took the state boards and passed all of the requirements. This was the first step for me to strengthen my sole and move forward in my nursing career.

I went back to work and transferred to another department. This expanded my knowledge even more as a Licensed Practical Nurse. In the new position, I assisted in training other new nurses. This gave me the opportunity to display my leadership skills. Eventually, I moved on and went to work for a large health insurance company, which further expanded my knowledge in that arena. It also provided me the opportunity to acquire knowledge of the administrative practices.

At this point in my life, I got married and had two more children. My husband and I raised the three boys in expectation of what God would have us do as a Christian family. However, this marriage did not work and we decided to go our separate ways. I raised the three boys as a single parent. I continued to work in the nursing field and when the opportunity arose I went back to school to advance my nursing education. That meant that on some days the children went with me to school and would study in the library's children's section while I was in class. We spent evenings together—I researched while they completed their homework. With strong determination, I graduated with an associate degree and again successfully passed the state nursing boards obtaining a license to practice as a registered nurse (RN). Throughout my career, I mentored many new nurses who went on to advance their skills and have successful careers.

I later established a very good relationship, remarried, and became a mother of two more boys in our blended family. Having a blended family was not easy but I took on the many awesome challenges wearing strong, solid shoes. As a military family, we lived overseas, which gave the family an opportunity to travel throughout Europe, even on a limited budget. I had to wear big shoes with spikes that allowed me to be a taxi mom, soccer mom, team mom, and nurse when sickness and injuries occurred. However, upon return to the United States and settling down, I went back to school to continue my nursing education. I obtained a Bachelor of Science degree in nursing. I eventually achieved a management position and successfully earned a Master of Science degree in Administration and Health Care Management. I also obtained a certification in Quality Assurance. I worked in this position until my retirement, which required good shoes with strong soles.

During my late adolescent and early adult life, I was able to make a connection with my biological parents. I can truly say that finding and identifying my biological mother and father impacted my life by helping me to overcome a feeling of abandonment. After meeting my mother, I realized that what she did was a true blessing for me. Seeing my mother's life situation made me understand that she did not have the ability to take care of another child as a single parent of four children. At first it was difficult to understand, but I convinced myself to believe that God had His hand in my destiny. My biological mother later assisted me in contacting my biological father when I was 21 years old. This was another big thing for me because for so many years I wondered about him and whether I would ever get the chance to meet him. We became close friends and I held no malice or ill thoughts towards either of my biological parents. I believed and trusted God for whatever would come of this relationship. This wonderful experience was like receiving a new pair of shoes, with a quality sole that helped to strengthen my foundation in life.

Now I am retired after a very successful career in the private sector and with the federal government. However, I am still very active in my church and I enjoy traveling, gardening, and reading. My goal is to leave a legacy for my family and friends to understand that whatever vision God places in your heart and soul can be accomplished through strong faith and dedication. Strive to reach your goals by working hard and maintaining your integrity and high moral standards. My motto is "Believe and you will achieve." Trust in God, for He knows your heart and mind and will guide your footsteps in whatever shoes you wear. I believe that God will always see us through in His own time. In addition, I believe it is very important to share and help others. The more you give to others in need, the more blessings will come to you. I trust that many people will say that I encouraged others during my walk through life. God's grace kept my vision alive. He allowed me to humbly pursue my dreams. I want to give thanks to my vocational instructor who saw me as a natural caregiver and who encouraged me to pursue the nursing career path.

As a final comment, I want to leave a message that there will always be sick people, who need healing, love, care and support. So if you have the compassion for the sick, seeking a nursing or medical career will be very rewarding. There are many different areas from which to choose, including administration, medical research, policy, quality management, and patient care. Nursing is my passion——what is yours? I will continue to leave a legacy of reaching back and helping others who desire a productive future and want to make a difference in society. I believe that I have made a difference in this world by serving God, country, and mankind. The world is a better place because I have shared my experiences and knowledge.

Part V

Fitted Shoes

CHAPTER 13

Do You Have a Good Fit?

A visiting minister to our church began his message with an analogy about Whitney Houston's life and early death. In my Toastmaster's club, we always stress how important it is to get an early attention grabber, if you are to capture your audience's attention at the onset. Well, the minister began by saying, "Whitney Houston thought she wasn't pretty enough. She thought she wasn't good enough. She wondered if people would like her!" The minister said these words were excerpts from the remarks given by screen actor Kevin Costner at Whitney's funeral.

Wow! If the late and great Whitney Houston had these kinds of doubts and fears, can you imagine how people feel, who actually may not be pretty in the eyes of man? Just think about those people, who won't be rich and famous in this lifetime. Also, think about those people, who aren't considered good enough to be at the table, where decisions are made. Many people would say that Whitney had it all. One of her last songs, I think, described her pain. The song is entitled, "I Didn't Know My Own Strength."

You see, we must allow God to come into our inner soul, not just into our minds; not just into our hearts; not just into our bodies but into our whole inner soul. This means allowing Him to live in us and through us. This means having God-consciousness in all that we say and in all that we do. This means allowing our soul to impact the steps of our sole, as we journey through life.

The minister I referred to earlier used as a subject for his message, "Living from the Inside Out." I found his message to be profound in so many ways. I could easily relate and I think many others could too. On our jobs, we feel the need to be competent, committed, courageous, caring, concerned, cooperative, commanding, and in control. We can easily become overwhelmed. There is an inner journey that corresponds to our outer life. If we are not prayerful, they can consume us. The struggle between the two causes us to lead a double existence, which can prove to be life threatening.

The journey can bring people into our lives who mean us no good. They can bring us down or get us hooked on things that destroy. On the other hand, this journey can bring wonderful people into our lives, people who are good role models and influence us to live lives that are pleasing to God.

The journey can bring challenges that require our faith to be tested. We need to surround ourselves with people who want what we want—and who serve who we serve. Specifically, we need like-minded people who want to please God and serve Him. If we do this, our outer life will reflect our inner journey. Just think, God loves us so much that He died for our sins. There is nothing too big for God to handle. We just have to learn how to lean and depend on Him. We need to be able to lay down our problems, issues, and concerns at the altar and leave them there.

If Whitney Houston, as beautiful and talented as she was, could feel insecure you can only imagine how many of us might feel the same way. Whitney had a powerful voice, which will leave a legacy in the music world. If we have not yet done so, each of us must discover our purpose so that we too can leave a legacy that lets the world know that we made a difference.

An example of living from the inside out was demonstrated to me when Mary Millben, a young woman who is a member of the Alfred Street Baptist Church Trinity Choir, made an appearance in June of 2013 at the "Cutting Ribbon" in New York City. Since Mary is one of "ours," we are especially proud of her. When she appeared on stage, I thought to myself—Isn't she lovely? Isn't she beautiful? Isn't she talented? And yes, she is "Working on Her Dream."

I am so proud to be a part of the Alfred Street Trinity Choir. I think we are awesome, as we go about serving God through music. Over eighty of us traveled to New York City to support our Mary. You see, Mary is an excellent example of "finding your shoes and wearing them." She captivated that New York audience wearing a beautiful black and white dress accented by 5-inch, sparkling red, open toe stilettos. She was stunning! The first song she performed, entitled, "I Am Working on My Dream," was written by music giant Bruce Springsteen. She also performed an original arrangement that appears on her CD and is now copyrighted. Mary's situation so epitomizes the spirit of *"Soul to Sole."* You see, first you need a dream. And remember, dreams are free. Dreams allow us to go places in our minds that we may or may not attain. But she also said she is "working" on her dream, which implies movement. Mary's got soul. There's no doubt about it. However, she uses her soles to travel along the highways and byways of life. She told us stories of her early beginnings in Oklahoma; about her travels to China and her internship at the White House during the George W. Bush administration. She shared with us her hunger for music that pushed her to transition from one set of shoes to another. Music is her dream—music is her passion. She knows and remembers that she can do all things through Christ who strengthens her. With her belief in God, her talent, charisma, and discipline, I see great things for Mary. She found her shoes and now she's walking in them.

Mary's example is one of finding your shoes, while pursuing wisdom. We must pray about everything and be anxious about nothing. When things seem to be going in an undesirable way, we must hit the pause button, reflect, and pray. I continue to find out that the Lord's Prayer is the best prayer there is. I especially remember . . . thou will be done . . . because GOD's will, will be done. I have found that if I pray in His will, I always end up in a good place. Many times, I end up in a better place than I imagined.

As you continue to read and enjoy *"Soul to Sole: The Views from the Shoes,"* ponder these questions: Do you have soul? What kind of soles are you wearing? Where is your soul going? Where are your soles taking you? Do you need to transition to soles that fit the life that God has preordained for you? Think about the shoes you want to best describe you—and make sure they are a good fit.

CHAPTER 14

Go Find Your Shoes

$\mathbf{D}$on't try to fill my shoes, go and find your own. However, in looking for and finding your shoes, seek the wisdom of God. I have heard, "As you get older, you get wiser." I have also heard, "There is no fool like an old fool." Proverbs 13:20, (KJV) says, "He that walketh with wise men shall be wise; but a companion of fools shall be destroyed."

As we travel on this road of life, we must learn to make wise decisions. We don't have to experience everything in life, especially the bad things. We can look at the missteps and wrong turns of others and set a trajectory that allows us to not make these same errors. When we are wise, we have a spirit of understanding, discernment, and sound judgment. Proverbs 3:13-15, (KJV) says, "Happy is the man that findeth wisdom, and the man that getteth understanding. For the merchandise of it is better than the merchandise of silver, and the gain thereof than fine gold."

Many have heard the motto of the United Negro College Fund, which says, "A mind is a terrible thing to waste." That is so true because the mind serves as our internal compass, leading and directing our thoughts and actions. It takes in data and information that may be Godly or worldly. That data can then be manipulated in such a way to control our responses to everyday situations. Our minds tell us what to do, when to do it, why we should do it, how we should do it, who we should do it with, and who we should do it to. So you see, this internal compass has a profound and powerful impact on our "soul" and our "soles." If we allow godly things to enter our minds, our feet are more likely to take us to godly places. On the other hand, if we allow worldly or secular things to enter our minds, our feet are likely to take us to worldly or secular places. My prayer is that God orders my steps, leads me, and guides me into the spaces and places that bring me closer to Him.

When you are looking for and finding your shoes, remember to ask God for wisdom. Ask Him to go before you and clear the pathway, so that you can stand firm and show discernment; so that you can walk by faith; so that you can run and not be weary; so that you can finish the race in God's time.

When you are looking for and finding your shoes, you will travel through all kinds of terrain. It is critical to keep a proper perspective. Wikipedia describes terrain as land relief. It further defines it as vertical and horizontal dimensions of the land surface. It says terrain is used as a general term in physical geography, referring to the lay of the land, which is usually expressed in terms of elevation, slope, and orientation of terrain features. Terrain affects surface water flow and distribution. Wikipedia goes on to say, over large areas, it can affect weather and climate patterns.

Understanding terrain is key to understanding "Soul to Sole: The Views from the Shoes" because this journey takes us on the road of life. We go through many seasons: winter, summer, spring, and fall. We experience tropical seasons, dry seasons, wet seasons, and storms. Some of us experience thunderstorms, lightning, tornadoes, and hurricanes. Some of us experience winter storms, blizzards, and firestorms. Sometimes we just see clouds. But then, there are the beautiful days when the sun shines bright with warmth and light. These are the days that make us want to be out and about. We forget about the dark clouds that held us back and the obstacles that were in our way. We look around and see the blue skies and know there is a God who sits high and looks low. We realize that He carries us through the sunshine and the rain and are grateful that He stands by us in our sorrow and in our pain.

As a retired Army officer, I relate the word "terrain" to navigation exercises that use maps and compasses. There are five major terrain features: hill, ridge, valley, saddle, and depression. I also think of the three minor terrain features: draw, spur, and cliff. It's amazing how the terrain analogy so perfectly fits life. We have high points in our lives, which motivate and inspire us and signify that we have made it to higher ground. What did it take to get there? Climbing those hills may have been hard. Climbing those hills may have caused many weary days and sleepless nights. However, once we reached the top, we could shout victory.

We also go through the ridges of life, where we reach a line of high ground but face height variations along the way. In other words, we are still striving to reach the top and have won a few battles although the war continues.

Then there are valleys, where we are surrounded by higher ground. The decision to make is whether to stay in the valley or try to climb one of the hills to see what's on the other side. While in the valley, we can trust in the "Lily of the Valley," who is our Lord and Savior Jesus Christ. We can seek His wisdom and guidance in leading us out of the valley into the marvelous light.

The saddles of life may keep on raging, as we try to move forward. These are low points along the crest of the ridge. We are trying to rise and stuff just keeps happening.

Depression in life is just like a hole in the ground. You feel like you are sinking deeper and deeper and there is no way out. Although you are surrounded by higher ground, it seems almost impossible to rise up; to look up or to even think about ever getting up.

When facing these five terrains we must remember that God can do for us what we cannot do for ourselves. He can take us to the hilltop of life as well as bring us through life's ridges, valleys, saddles, and depressions. God can do any and all things. If God is for us, then who can be against us?

In one of his sermons, my pastor said, "We must let go of the natural feelings and embrace our righteous mind." To me, that means we cannot always respond to how we feel, because feelings come and go. For example, many people want to be happy. And, happiness can be good. However, happiness is dependent on others. Your family, relatives, friends, associates, and even enemies affect your happiness. I suggest you seek joy, which is from God. Joy exceeds happiness. Joy is deep down in your soul and it springs hope eternal. Joy helps you to smile when you really want to cry. Joy helps you to focus on the things for which you are thankful. A righteous mind is one that is stayed on Jesus. It directs your talk and it directs your walk. By embracing a righteous mind, we choose to follow Jesus. We choose to love the Lord with all our heart, mind, and soul.

Christ is the wisdom of God and this wisdom is available to each of us. Because the Holy Spirit resides in us, we are victorious. As 1 John 4:4 (KJV) says, "Ye are of God, little children, and have overcome them: because greater is He that is in you than he that is in the world."

GO FIND YOUR SHOES . . .
AND MAKE SURE THEY ARE THE RIGHT FIT.

CONCLUSION

Writing *Soul to Sole: The Views from the Shoes* was a true labor of love. It afforded my aging mother an opportunity to narrate her story, as I captured it, so that it can be a part of her legacy. She and I both enjoy writing poems, so this work presented the perfect opportunity to inject our poetry. This work allowed Gil, Summer, and I to bond even more, as we reflected upon some of our life experiences. It presented an opportunity to share the challenges and joys of caring for a senior. And, this effort allowed us to expand our circle of love to incorporate contributions from other women, who love and serve God.

Throughout the book, I make reference to my pastor, Reverend Howard John Wesley, Pastor of Alfred Street Baptist Church in Alexandria, Virginia. He always says, "Read your bible. It will make you a better Christian." I am a witness to that, as I have chosen to read a scripture every night before I go to bed. Then, every morning upon my rising, I say my prayers and read a scripture before I start my day. My girlfriend, Gale, gave me a wonderful devotional journal for every day of the year entitled, "Jesus Calling: Enjoying Peace in His Presence" by Sarah Young. I have found this to be a great addition to my daily devotions. This habit of reading my bible daily allows me to purposely focus on God's word and become more knowledgeable of His will.

Soul to Sole targets girls and women. I think the biblical story of Mary and Martha is a great example of the complexities of sisterhood. Sometimes we are too busy with the hustle and bustle of our daily activities that we do not find time to sit at Jesus' feet. And, when we do, we must remember not to skimp on our time with the Lord. Whether we are related by the blood of our parents or the blood of Jesus, all girls and women are sisters. We need to share sisterly love and spend quality time in the presence of God and in fellowship with each other.

The contributors to this book pour out their hearts, in hopes of inspiring and/or motivating girls and women. The bible teaches that nothing is born without an act of intimacy. It is my hope that this book will help explain the need for an intimate relationship with God and encourage you to trust and obey Him. As you walk through life, experiencing all the joys and sorrows that will come— Remember to seek wisdom, as you find and wear your fitted shoes.

EPILOGUE

By
Dr. Mabel Jones Matthews

"Pausing To Take Our Souls and Soles to the Repair Shop"

As we proceed through life's spiritual and physical walks, we stroll down pathways; we cross mountains, clear obstacles, and jog highways that are rocky and occasionally cruel. Sometimes these challenges wear down our soul and our soles. But remember, James 1:2-4 (KJV) *"My brethren, count it all joy when ye fall into divers temptations; knowing this, that the trying of your faith worketh patience. But let patience have her perfect work, that ye may be perfect and entire, wanting nothing."* So how might we ready ourselves for endurance? We pause to take our soul and soles to the repair shop.

Though our spiritual souls need to be built on a strong foundation of godly faith, love, worship and praise, so too, our shoe soles need to be girded with good leather, arch support, beauty and a comfortable fit. The soul and the sole complement each other while guiding us through our daily journeys.

When weary and worn, do not turn your soul nor sole over to just anyone for restoration. Seek a professional whom God has given the

187

gifts and talents of retooling souls and soles; seek one who is led by the Holy Spirit and scholarly prepared to be a restorer of souls; seek one who has been trained in the skillful art of shoe repair and values the awesome splendor of sole restoration.

As we head to the repair shop for our soul we must seriously commit to bible study, prayer and meditation; counseling and mentoring; therapy and networking—not forgetting worship and praise. For our soles, we observe those with well-fitted shoes, which lack run over heels and holes in the sole. We seek their advice and head to these highly recommended shoe repair shops. We head to the soul and sole repair shops before damaging holes are formed. We reach out for restoration early, so that our souls and soles will remain intact. There will be no fading of beauty and weakening of our foundation. An early visit allows us to be lifted up, resoled, shined, polished, refined, replenished, glorified and restored to our "true purpose"—a godly walk with Christ.

The ultimate beauty of pausing to take our souls and soles to the repair shop is that we can. God gives us the gift of restoration that replenishes our souls and soles for the journey. To God be the Glory, for the foundation of *"Soul to Sole"* and Mrs. Lucille Brown Floyd. May God continue to shower her with His mighty favor.

"Take my yoke upon you, and learn of me;
for I am meek and lowly in heart; and ye shall
find rest unto your souls."

Matthew 11:29 (KJV)

ANNEX OF ADDITIONAL POEMS

God Brought Me

By
Lucille B. Floyd

God brought me from a mighty long way,
and with Him, I will always stay.
He is my rock, my sword, and my shield,
He is my wheel in the middle of a wheel.
So bow your head and say a little prayer,
because my great God is always near.

My Jesus Is Enough

By
Lucille Floyd

Oh, the sweet name of Jesus,
gentle Savior gives me hope.
He is my strength and security,
my friend to help me cope.
Life isn't always easy,
and my path is sometimes rough.
But I have found real joy and peace,
for my Jesus is enough.

When days are dark and burdened,
and when fear wants to console.
Friends may not be faithful,
and no one may be there for me to hold.
Disappointments may threaten me.
But I just look to Jesus,
and allow him my strength to be.

The Lord is my strength and shield,
in whom my heart trusted and found help.
So, my heart rejoices, with my song.
I praise my God all the day long.

September's Child

By
Carolyn Knowles

She was born on a brisk day, in the month of September.
The drama she experienced, she would always remember.
She was unwanted and unloved, by her real mom and dad.
But, at least she was not aborted, and for that she was glad.

What others meant for bad, God meant for good.
And, as she grew older, she finally understood.
Her blood relatives chose to throw her away.
But, she proved to be a survivor from that very first day.

She was born with a veil, which covered her entire face.
It made her stand out, as a unique and special case.
She was able to see things, which others could not.
This caused her to frighten easily, especially as a little tot.

She went through life, making mistakes along the way.
But, she always showed love and kindness, each and every day.
It was nothing for her to give her last to another.
This was demonstrated with her step sisters,
step brothers, and mothers.
Yes, mothers—her step mother and real mother too,
She ended up caring for both of them,
as it was the right thing to do.

The years have gone by and she is now old.
But, her story is one that had to be told.
She passed the torch to another generation.
She challenged them to wait on the Lord,
trust, and hope—with great expectation.

She reflected on her life, as she looked back and smiled.
She thanked God Almighty for His September's Child.

Let Wisdom Reign

By
Carolyn Knowles
(Inspired by Martin Luther King Jr.'s
"I Have a Dream" Speech)

When there is a decision to be made or a course to be run,
Let Wisdom Reign.
When there is trouble in the air and problems everywhere,
Let Wisdom Reign.

Wisdom is not for the meek and the timid.
Wisdom is not for the fearful or the shy.
Wisdom is for those who will be strong and courageous,
even until the day that they die.

Wisdom is for those, who will trust and obey.
Wisdom is for those, who will serve Jesus, each and every day.

Let wisdom reign in all of our terrain.
Let it reign in our mountains of hope.
Let it reign in our valleys of despair.
Let it reign along the ridges of ridicule.
Let it reign along the saddles of humiliation.
Let it reign in the spurs of insensitivity.
Let it reign in the hilltops of happiness.
Let Wisdom Reign.

When we let wisdom reign,
we will be in God—and God will be in us.
When we let wisdom reign,
our decisions will be made with discernment.
Our paths will be trod with joy.

**Let Wisdom Reign . . . Let Wisdom
Reign . . . Let Wisdom Reign**

Perspectives

By
Carolyn Knowles

Perspectives . . . We all have them.
They are our thoughts and opinions.
They are our concepts and ideas.
They can be the impetus for our fears.
They can be the cause of our tears.

We can choose to see the glass half empty.
Or, we can choose to see the glass half full.
We can choose to see sunshine after the rain.
Or, we can choose to feel joy after our pain.

We can choose to sigh, with each and every breath we take.
We can choose to complain, with each and every step we make.
Or, we can choose to love life and accept all that it brings,
knowing that through Christ, we can do all things.

We can choose to focus on the dark clouds and grey skies.
Or, we can choose to keep hope alive, as we continue to rise.
We can build a firm foundation that is built on Jesus Christ,
our Lord and our Savior, who paid the ultimate price.

Perspectives . . . We all have them.
They are our thoughts and opinions.
They are our concepts and ideas.
They can be the impetus for our fears.
They can be the cause of our tears.